About the Book

Was Douglas MacArthur the greatest general in American history? Was he only a vain actor who spent his life wearing a uniform to appease his wish for self-drama? The truth, as John Devaney reveals in this incisive biography, lies somewhere between the extremes.

MacArthur sometimes seemed the stuff of Hollywood. But he lived and helped shape the course of history in the first half of this century as did few other men. In this book Devaney shows him as viewed by intimate friends and bitter enemies from his earliest days as the son of a U.S. general who had been a hero in the Civil War. Perhaps MacArthur was trying to prove he was as great a man as his father. If that was so, he certainly succeeded.

Here we see him in his first great adventure in Mexico before he became a front-line hero on the Western Front in World War I. As the nation's Army Chief of Staff he chased the Bonus Marchers out of Washington in the Depression 1930s, then went on to try to organize an army for the government of the Philippines. The outbreak of World War II caught him off guard, but he returned to retake the Philippines and become the benign occupation head of defeated Japan. Finally came the Korean War, and a great victory and a great disaster for MacArthur personally. This absorbing biography shows that wherever the General went, controversy and adventure accompanied him.

DOUGLAS MacARTHUR

Something of a Hero

by John Devaney

G. P. PUTNAM'S SONS, NEW YORK

*For a man to succeed in a democracy he must be
something of a saint and something of a hero.*
—GEORGE SANTAYANA

Library of Congress Cataloging in Publication Data
Devaney, John.
Douglas MacArthur, something of a hero.
Includes index.
SUMMARY: A biography of the controversial general
with emphasis on his service during the two World Wars
and the Korean War.
1. MacArthur, Douglas, 1880-1964—Juvenile literature.
2. Generals—United States—Biography—Juvenile
literature. [1. MacArthur, Douglas, 1880-1964.
2. Generals] I. Title.
U53.M25D48   355.3'31'0924   [92]   [B]   78-10820
ISBN 0-399-20660-4

All photos from the National Archives

For Grant Esposito, whose best player was
Luke Devaney, and to Jeff Jordan's (J.J.'s) team, and
to Carmen Edgerly and Miss Lewin of P.S. 41,
and to June 25, 1968—the happiest day of Luke's life.

Contents

Acknowledgments

I am indebted to several dozen writers whose newspaper articles, magazine pieces and books on MacArthur have been the major sources for what I have put into this biography. By far the best balanced and most thorough work on MacArthur is D. Clayton James' two-volume biography, *The Years of MacArthur* (a third volume is scheduled to cover the years from 1945 until his death).

Much of the material on MacArthur can be divided into two parts: books that are almost unashamed in their reverence for the man; and books that are either critical or, at best, unfriendly. Among the reverent books are Frazier Hunt's *The Untold Story of Douglas MacArthur*, Courtney Whitney's *MacArthur: Rendevouz with Destiny*, and Charles A. Willoughby's *MacArthur, 1941–1951*, written with John Chamberlain. And there is MacArthur's autobiography, *Reminiscences*, put together near the end of his life with the obvious assistance of Whitney, Willoughby, and others.

Of the books that are critical toward MacArthur, a highly readable one in paperback is Clay Blair, Jr.'s *MacArthur*. I would also recommend Gavin Long's *MacArthur as Military Commander*.

Books that were written earlier in MacArthur's career, when he was less controversial a figure, include John Hersey's *Men on Bataan*. And Clark Lee's and Richard Henschel's *Douglas MacArthur* tries to give a balanced view of the man, especially during his years in the Philippines before and just after the war. A valuable look at MacArthur when he was the superintendent at West Point is contained in William A. Ganoe's *MacArthur Close-up*.

I am indebted to a long list of writers who have left portraits of MacArthur in newspaper and magazine articles, notably in *The New York Times, Colliers, Saturday Evening Post, Time, Newsweek, Readers Digest* and *Esquire*. For his help during a fruitful visit to West Point I thank Kenneth W. Rapp, Assistant Archivist, USMA Archives. I owe thanks to my wife, Barbara, for her diligent interviews of several sources, especially Fred DaTorre.

———J.D.

DOUGLAS MacARTHUR

Something of a Hero

1

"The Boy Lieutenant"

The General's hawkish profile was etched against the glow of the match for a moment as he lit his pipe. The General, his figure as erect as a flagpole, stood in the shadows on this night of December 7, 1941, a date Americans would never forget.

He stood on a terrace high above the glittering city of Manila, "the Pearl of the Orient." From the terrace General Douglas MacArthur could see an island in Manila Bay called Corregidor. And beyond that island, like a fat thumb jutting into Manila Bay, loomed a largely jungle peninsula called Bataan.

Bataan. Corregidor. They were names unknown to most Americans on this night of December 7, 1941. But at this moment—amid the shrill shouts of "Banzai!"—Japanese bombers were rising off aircraft carriers in the Pacific some five thousand miles from where MacArthur stood. They droned in the pink early morning light toward American battleships in Pearl Harbor in Hawaii. Soon the names Bataan and Corregidor—and Douglas MacArthur—would inspire Americans with emotions of hope. After hope would come despair and defeat, the worst in the history of the U.S. Army.

13

The guns of World War II would soon thunder across the Pacific, but on this warm and serene night in Manila, as he puffed his pipe, General Douglas MacArthur had reason to think—as he often did—of his father, General Arthur MacArthur. As one of the commanders of an American army, General Arthur MacArthur marched into Manila in 1898. Arthur MacArthur later became the first military commander of the Filipinos and their thousand-island nation, the Philippines, which became a U.S. possession.

Standing alone on the dark terrace, General Douglas MacArthur could tell himself that he had matched the military record of the general-father he idolized Almost. But not completely. His father had attained an honor that twice had been in Douglas MacArthur's grasp—and twice had eluded that grasp. That was the Congressional Medal of Honor, America's highest award to its heroes. The Congressional Medal of Honor had been won by Arthur MacArthur, "the Boy Lieutenant" as he was called, during America's bloody war between the states at a place in Tennessee called Missionary Ridge.

The date was November 25, 1863. The 24th Wisconsin Volunteer Infantry Regiment rushed across the open field as Confederate bullets tore into chests and musket balls shattered boyish faces. Blue-clad Union soldiers, huge holes in their chests and backs, were strewn over the field and their flowing blood darkened the grass.

Leading the charge of the 24th Wisconsin was eighteen-year-old Lieutenant Arthur MacArthur. Amid shouts of the regiment's rallying cry—"On, Wisconsin!"—and the rattle and roar of battle, the Boy Lieutenant led his troops—their bayonets flashing—into the Confederate rifle pits at the bottom of Missionary Ridge. For several minutes there was fierce hand-to-hand fighting. Several times the blue line wavered. But each time it pushed forward, finally ejecting the gray-uniformed Confederates, who fled up the rocky, gullied hill toward its top at Missionary Ridge.

From the ridge the Confederate cannon lobbed shells at the

14

Union troops huddled in the rifle pits. "We can't live here! We must go forward!" shouted Lieutenant MacArthur. His face was blackened by gunpowder and glistened with sweat.

Up the hill swept the 24th Wisconsin, stumbling over the broken ground and the bodies of dead or dying men. "It was more of a climb than a charge," one Wisconsin trooper later recalled. Coughing, gasping, cursing soldiers heard balls of iron whiz by their heads. Men were blown backward and rolled down the hill, legs and arms shot away. But upward the ragged blue line climbed toward Missionary Ridge.

Near the top of the hill the 24th Wisconsin's color bearer fell. Amid the twisting ravines on the hill the 24th soldiers stopped, not knowing—without a color bearer—where to rally round for a concentrated assault. Confederate marksmen picked them off where they stood and for several moments the soldiers seemed poised to turn their backs and race down the hill.

Lieutenant MacArthur seized the fallen staff and waved the colors. The 24th's soldiers rushed to the Boy Lieutenant as he darted forward into the center of the Confederate line on Missionary Ridge. Seeing the fluttering colors, some sixty other battle-flag carriers raced toward it, followed by the survivors of this mad charge. Because the slope was so steep at this point on Missionary Ridge, the Confederate cannonballs flew over the heads of the 24th's charging troops.

The lieutenant, waving the colors, swept into the entrenched Confederates. A Confederate captain swung his saber, but a bullet struck the blade, deflecting it, and the saber only ripped off the lieutenant's shoulder strap.

For several minutes the center of Missionary Ridge was a scrambled mass of blue and gray. Then, like a giant heaving a huge log, the Union troops threw the Confederates off the hill. From nearby hills, watching the action, came roars from the rest of the Union Army.

15

"For coolness and conspicuous bravery in action," the citation would read, "in seizing the colors of his regiment at a critical moment and planting them on the captured works on the crest of Missionary Ridge, Tennessee," First Lieutenant Arthur MacArthur was awarded the Congressional Medal of Honor.

A year later, at only nineteen, he became a colonel, the youngest in the Union Army. Twice he was badly wounded, but he survived to lead the 24th Wisconsin Regiment as it marched back to its home town of Milwaukee at the war's end in 1865.

Young MacArthur left the Army and, to the delight of his father, a prominent Milwaukee judge, began to study law. But he could not forget the sounds of battle. In 1866 he rejoined the Army as a second lieutenant. He was soon promoted to captain, a commander of troops on the Western plains, where the Army fought marauding Apaches and chased outlaws like Jesse James and Billy the Kid.

In 1874 Arthur MacArthur was transferred to New Orleans where the captain met a southern belle, Mary Pinkney Hardy—"Pinky" to her friends. She became his wife. Their first child, Arthur, was born two years later. A second son, Malcolm, was born in 1878 but died of measles when he was five. On January 26, 1880, a third son was born in Little Rock, Arkansas, where Captain MacArthur was the commander of Company K of the 13th Infantry. This son was named Douglas.

The five-month-old Douglas, bundled in his mother's arms, went west by train with Company K in May, 1880. Company K was first assigned to guard Fort Wingate on the windy plains of New Mexico, then—when Douglas was four—to Fort Selden, Texas. It watched the winding Rio Grande River to attempt to block any move by Geronimo, the Apache chief, to cross into Mexico.

Young Douglas' first memory was the three-hundred-mile march from Fort Wingate to Fort Selden. He and his brother, Arthur, often trudged at the head of the column with First Sergeant Peter Ripley. One day, as the thirsty soldiers tramped along a hot trail, they met a rancher. Sergeant Ripley—with Douglas and Arthur at his side— asked the rancher, "How far to the next water hole?"

"About ten miles," said the rancher.

Some three hours later the column of troops still sought that elusive water hole. They met another rancher. "How far to the next water hole?" asked Sergeant Ripley, panting.

"About ten miles."

Sergeant Ripley turned and shouted at the dry-throated men behind him: "It's all right, boys. Thank God we're holding our own."

At Fort Selden Douglas rode with the troops. "I learned to ride and shoot before I could walk and talk," he often said, with some exaggeration. But he awoke each morning as bugle calls pierced the air and he galloped each afternoon across the broad plains on his own pinto. And at night he often confided to his mother that he wanted to be just like his father: an Army officer who roamed the frontier to fight the Apache and Sioux.

In 1889, much to the nine-year-old Douglas' disappointment, his father was transferred east to Washington. Arthur MacArthur, now a major, was assigned to the Adjutant General's Department, the personnel and management branch of the Army.

Pinky MacArthur—a woman raised in the genteel ways of the South—must have been overjoyed after years of log-cabin life on the frontier. Now her children would get a proper education instead of being taught in ramshackle schoolhouses on Army outposts. She and her two sons were especially close. The loss of Malcolm, MacArthur once said, "was a terrible blow to my mother, but it seemed only to increase her devotion to Arthur and myself. This tie was to become one of the dominant factors of my life."

For the next four years Douglas attended the Force Public School on Washington's Massachusetts Avenue. For much of those years he day dreamed of the plains, ponies and bugle calls of a frontier post. In 1893 he graduated, "only" he later admitted, "an average student."

His brother, Arthur, unable to get an appointment to the United States Military Academy at West Point, had been admitted to the United States Naval Academy at Annapolis. In 1896 he graduated as an ensign and would soon become one of the Navy's first submarine commanders.

When Douglas was fourteen, his father was sent back to the West. At Fort Sam Houston in San Antonio, Texas, the fourteen-year-old Douglas again played happily amid the sounds he loved: the barked orders of the parade grounds, the crackle and roar of the firing range.

He attended the West Texas Military Academy. That school's military atmosphere, mixed with the boy's delight at being back on the frontier, ignited a flame. "This is where I started . . ." he would later write in his *Reminiscenses*. "There came a desire to know, a seeking for the reason why, a search for the truth." Almost overnight an average boy became a brilliant one.

Yet he was no bookworm. A wiry hundred thirty pounds, he was the quarterback for the school's football team in his last year. During the fierce scrimmages, "you could see his lips turn blue," a teammate once recalled. "But he would get up and fight again. I know all the boys believed in him." He was the school's top tennis player, the shortstop of the baseball team and its best bunter.

He graduated in 1897 as the class valedictorian, his average in his last year an almost perfect 97.53. His father wrote to get recommendations so his son could enter West Point by presidential appointment. This did not occur, but a Milwaukee Congressman wired the old Civil War hero, now a lieutenant colonel, that there would be a test in his district in the spring of 1898. Dozens of Milwaukee boys would take the test; only one would be admitted.

Douglas and his mother moved to Milwaukee, where he spent some six months of intensive study. His father, meanwhile, was again caught up in a swirl of battle. America was at war with Spain after an American battleship, the *Maine*, had been blown up in Havana, Cuba, then a Spanish possession. Promoted to brigadier general, Arthur MacArthur landed near Manila on July 31, 1898, to

18

join the American Army sent to conquer the Spanish colony of which that city was the capital. In the Philippines he found a letter from Douglas, who begged to be allowed to enlist in the Army as a private. "My son," the general wrote back, "there will be plenty of fighting in the coming years, and of a magnitude far beyond this. Prepare yourself."

The scholarly Arthur MacArthur, an avid reader, had come to realize what few Americans did at that time. In the dawning Twentieth Century, America would be drawn out of its isolation to become embroiled in the wars that have always raged among world powers.

In the Philippines the American Army shortly overwhelmed the Spanish garrison. But the people of the Philippines then revolted as they demanded independence. Their principal leader, Emilio Aguinaldo, led a guerrilla army that began to battle the Americans on Luzon, the largest of the islands, early in 1899. Fighting raged even in the streets of Manila. In 1901 President McKinley appointed Arthur MacArthur, now a major general, as the American military commander of the Philippines, his job to suppress the rebels. Learning of his father's rise to fame, young Douglas had no way of knowing that one day he would also command another defeated Asian people.

Before these faraway events, as he prepared for the West Point test, Douglas felt his stomach churn. He worried that he would fail. Then he couldn't attain his father's fame. The night before the test he tossed and turned, unable to sleep. The next morning, as he arrived with his mother at the building where the test would be held, he feared he would vomit on the steps.

His mother stopped him as they walked up the steps. She put a hand on his shoulder. "Douglas," she said, "you'll win if you don't lose your nerve. You must believe in yourself, my son, or no one else will believe in you. Be self-confident, self-reliant, and even if you don't make it, you will know you have done your best."

In the test he got a mark of 93.3. His nearest competitor had a 77.

On a warm June day in 1899, Cadet Douglas MacArthur and his mother stepped off a railroad car and saw, for the first time, the fog-gray stone buildings of West Point that towered over the Hudson River.

MacArthur walked through the gates of West Point toward the flat Plain where he would march with the long gray line of cadets for the next four years. But soon he would have to face a stoney-faced judge who would ask him a question he would refuse to answer. That refusal, he knew, could mean the end of all his boyish dreams.

2

"Not to Strip Me of My Uniform"

"Step into the tent, Cadet MacArthur!"

The tense, nineteen-year-old plebe, erect in his high-collared gray uniform, shouldered his way through the canvas flaps. Sitting on cots, grinning, were about a dozen upperclassmen.

MacArthur stood stiffly at attention. From the dark woods nearby came the chatter of crickets. As part of the plebes' summer-long introduction to West Point, they had to go through what was called "Beast Barracks." The upperclassmen were allowed to "exercise" the plebes. They could order them to do silly things like stand on a chair and sing or make them crawl on the floor like turtles. The upperclassmen were forbidden to be cruel to the plebes—but often were. Each summer dozens of plebes limped away from the hazings of Beast Barracks with aching legs and arms.

MacArthur had been singled out for special hazings. First of all, he stood out among the other plebes: practically six feet tall, slender, with flashing dark eyes. Fellow cadet Robert E. Wood later said he was "the handsomest cadet that ever came into the academy." Secondly, he was the son of Arthur MacArthur, that famous general who was fighting the Filipino rebel army led by Aguinaldo. "We always prepared a warm reception for the sons of well-known men," Cadet Wood later said, "and the well-known man in this instance was General Arthur MacArthur."

An upperclassman ordered MacArthur to do "spread eagles." He had to squat and rise while waving his arms. MacArthur did two hundred fifty eagles before he was allowed to stop, his face white. Then he had to hang by his hands from a tent pole for two minutes. His shoulders and arms ached and sweat streamed down his face and back. For another hour he had to do pushups.

Dismissed at last, MacArthur staggered back to his tent on wobbly legs. He opened the flap of the tent and pitched face-first onto the wooden floor. He couldn't stand. A fellow plebe, Fred Cunningham, tried to lift him. MacArthur's arms and legs thrashed wildly out of control. His feet and hands banged against the floor boards.

In a hoarse voice MacArthur pleaded with Cunningham to put a blanket under him to cushion the banging sounds. He didn't want a passing officer to hear. He could order MacArthur to tell what had happened. If his hazers were caught, they would be expelled. For the rest of the night MacArthur twisted and turned in agony on the floor, a corner of the blanket stuffed into his mouth to suppress his moans.

The next morning MacArthur reported for formation, bedsheet pale. Other plebes begged him to go on sick call. He refused. In the sticky-hot morning and all afternoon he marched with his company under the blaze of an August sun.

Word of MacArthur's hazing—and what it had done to him— spread through the three-hundred-twenty-two-man corps of cadets. The upperclassmen who had hazed him were frightened that they would be expelled. That next evening they came to MacArthur's tent and, one by one, thanked him for his silence.

A year later, though, a cadet was severely injured during a hazing and later died. At the insistence of President William McKinley, a military court of inquiry was appointed to investigate West Point hazing. The court learned of MacArthur's hazing and ordered him to testify. Under oath he was asked by a judge to name the cadets who had hazed him.

MacArthur swallowed hard. Years later he described the conflict that raged within him:

"If the court insisted and ordered me to reveal the names, and I refused to obey the order, it would in all likelihood mean my dismissal and the end of all my hopes and dreams. It would be so easy and expedient to yield, to tell, and who would blame me?"

But he knew what his mother and his father, far away in the Philippines, would say: "Don't be a tattletale." During a court recess he received a poem his mother had written to him that ended with the words: "She reaps as she sowed. 'This man is her son!' "

"I knew then what to do," MacArthur wrote in *Reminiscences*. "Come what may, I would be no tattletale."

In the courtroom MacArthur again was told to reveal the names. Staring at the judge, MacArthur said he could not. He was willing, he said, to accept any punishment for failing to obey the order—anything, he said, "but not to strip me of my uniform."

The judge stared at the erect, pale cadet. "Court is recessed," he said. "Take him to his quarters."

For the next few hours MacArthur paced the small room he shared with another cadet. When he heard footsteps in the hall, he stopped. His heart pounded. He awaited a knock on the door and the word that he had been expelled.

The knock never came. The judges got the names of the hazers from someone else. MacArthur was allowed to go back to his classrooms.

He was doing astonishingly well in those classrooms. His roommate, an upperclassman, Arthur Hyde, called him "one of the hardest working men I have ever known . . . his every energy was directed to the attainment of . . . number one in his class."

To Arthur Hyde, young MacArthur talked of the pride he felt in being the son of General MacArthur. He told Hyde how his father had commanded a regiment before he was twenty-one, a full colonel, and how he had won that most cherished of awards—the Congressional Medal of Honor. He felt a burden weighing on his shoulders, he told Hyde, to be "a worthy successor" to his father.

In his first year MacArthur studied math, English, French and drill regulations. He finished first in his class of a hundred thirty-four in math, first in English, second in French and first in drill. Watching MacArthur strut on a parade ground, snapping out orders to a platoon of plebes, a West Point captain said to another officer: "There's the finest drillmaster I have ever seen."

On weekends girls visited West Point from nearby cities, attending cadet dances, or "hops" as they were called. One of MacArthur's dates at a hop was Bess Follansbee of New York City. The night after the dance Bess wrote this in her diary of MacArthur: "I liked him immensely and thought him a splendid dancer. He is tall, slim, dark, with a very bright, pleasant manner."

The next afternoon Bess and her girl friends strolled to the hotel where Mrs. MacArthur lived. MacArthur and his cadet friends soon appeared. The cadets weren't supposed to be there without written permission. But they chatted with the girls in front of a cast-iron, big bellied stove.

There was a quick knocking on the door. MacArthur opened it. Outside was his mother. She whispered to him that a West Point officer had just entered the hotel. The boys had better hide.

Grabbing their overcoats, the cadets scuttled out of the room and dashed down the stairs to the cellar, where they hid. Their "eyes"—Pinky MacArthur—watched the officer talk to a guest, then leave. When she was sure the officer was gone, she called to the cadets. Back upstairs they enjoyed another hour of conversation with the girls before time came for the visitors to depart—by horse and carriage or river boat—for New York.

The lanky MacArthur, with a hundred forty pounds now strung on his near six-foot frame, tried out for the West Point baseball team and made the "nine," as baseball teams were then called. "He was far from brilliant," the team's captain said some fifty years later, "but somehow he could manage to get on first. He'd outfox the pitcher, draw a base on balls, or get a single, or outrun a bunt—and there he'd be on first."

MacArthur stood in left field for Army on a warm and cloudy afternoon in 1901 when Army played Navy—the first baseball games ever between the two schools. In the splintery bleachers the Navy rooters tried to rattle MacArthur. They teased the famous general's son about his father's inability to capture the wily rebel leader.

> Are you the Governor General
> Or a hobo?
> Who is the boss of this show?
> Is it you or Emilio Aguinaldo?

The Navy rooters roared derisive laughter. But MacArthur had the last laugh. With the score tied 3–3, he squirmed and twisted in the batter's box, making himself as small a target for the pitcher as he could. He drew a walk.

He trotted to first base. Behind him the Navy catcher was arguing with the umpire about the last pitch being called a ball. MacArthur figured the catcher might be upset by that call.

On the first pitch to the next hitter, MacArthur streaked for second. "Sure enough," he said later, "the catcher threw wild." MacArthur flew around second and dashed for third. An outfielder picked up the bounding ball, threw toward third, but the ball bulleted over the third baseman's head. MacArthur raced home with the run that beat Navy, 4–3.

For an Army–Navy football game, or some other occasion, the Corps of Cadets might leave what they called 'the Monastery on the Hudson" for a weekend of freedom in New York or Philadelphia.

25

Once, after attending a horse show, MacArthur and two other cadets walked into Rector's, then a famous restaurant on Manhattan's Broadway.

They told the bartender to serve them nine martinis.

The bartender stared. "There's only three of you," he said. "Where are the other six?"

"Their spirits are here," shouted one, and then, leaving the drinks untouched, they "swanked out to a burlesque show," MacArthur recalled. "We loved it!"

There were few such hijinks for the serious-minded MacArthur, intent on being No. 1 in his class. He was No. 1 in his first and second years but dropped to No. 4 in his third year.

Once he failed to take several math tests because he was in the hospital for a checkup. Although he was the best student in the class, he saw his name listed as a "goat," which meant he had to take the final exam.

MacArthur called on his math professor, an almost unheard-of thing for a cadet to do. MacArthur was almost insubordinate as he argued with the professor that his scores on other tests excused him from the final. He demanded that his name be taken off the list of "goats."

That night MacArthur told his roommate at the time: "I will not take that test. I know it is an order, but it is an unreasonable one." Then he added: "If my name is not off that list before nine in the morning, I'll resign!"

"But what will your father say?"

"He will be terribly disappointed. But I believe he will see my attitude in the matter and approve my action."

At ten minutes to nine the next morning a new order was posted. The understanding professor had been swayed by MacArthur's arguments. His name was off the goat list.

MacArthur, for the first time but not for the last, had looked the authority of the Army in the eyes and walked away the victor.

At the start of MacArthur's senior year he was named to the highest post of any West Point cadet: First Captain of the Corps. He gave up playing baseball and being manager of the football team to focus all his attention on books. That year he was the first in his class in law, history, gunnery and military efficiency, third in engineering, fourth in drill, fifth in soldierly deportment, tenth in conduct and thirty-seventh in military engineering. He was once again No. 1 in his class. He would graduate with a four-year average of 98.14, the highest of any cadet in twenty-five years.

On a bright June morning in 1903 MacArthur sat stiffly on a wooden chair on the green West Point Plain. On a stage Secretary of War Elihu Root addressed the graduating cadets and their proud parents.

Among those parents were Pinky and Arthur MacArthur. General MacArthur had captured Emilio Aguinaldo and ended the Filipino uprising. Then, with a series of warm and humane edicts, he had begun to win the respect of the Filipinos. This MacArthur, Filipinos said, was a white face they could trust. But MacArthur had quarreled with a civilian politician sent to oversee the military commander. The President sided with the civilian, William Howard Taft, who would himself soon become President of the United States. MacArthur had been ordered to command troops in Colorado, a demotion that embittered him toward politicians. Some fifty years later his son would have a far more sensational confrontation with another President.

"Before you leave the Army," Elihu Root told the ninety-four new second lieutenants assembled before him at the graduation ceremony, "according to all precedents in our history, you will be engaged in another war. It is bound to come and will come. Prepare your country for that war."

A little later, as the graduating cadets stood in a long line, an officer called out the name of the No. 1 cadet in the class: "Douglas MacArthur!"

Amid applause MacArthur walked forward and accepted his

diploma and gold bars. He was now a second lieutenant of the Corps of Engineers. MacArthur strode quickly up a long aisle to where his mother and father sat. With a bow, he handed the diploma to the father he revered.

He had given his father what Arthur MacArthur had never had the chance to win—a West Point commission. Now he could be the general his father was. That opportunity would come, for massing over Europe were the dark clouds of the war that Elihu Root had predicted would come.

3

Behind the Mexican Lines

Captain Douglas MacArthur stared for several moments at the mustached Mexican. Then he asked: "Are you sure that the locomotives are there?"

The Mexican nodded vigorously. "I am sure they are in the town of Alvardio, Captain. I can take you to them. But I must be paid."

MacArthur handed the Mexican several gold pieces. "If you take me to the locomotives and bring me back here unharmed to Veracruz," he said, "you will be paid another one hundred dollars."

"Agreed, señor."

MacArthur and the Mexican were standing in a dark alley in the city of Veracruz on a warm May evening in 1914. Since his graduation from West Point eleven years earlier, MacArthur had risen to captain. His first assignment had been to the Philippines, where the name MacArthur was famous. He had landed at the port of Tacloban on the island of Leyte. As part of an engineering battalion, he had drawn maps of trails in the thick jungles of a peninsula on Luzon called Bataan. He helped to arm a fortress island in Manila Bay called Corregidor.

For the next year, 1904, he had joined his father, now a lieutenant general and the highest-ranking officer in the U.S. Army, on an official tour of the Orient. The father and son, with Mrs. MacArthur, visited Japan and observed the war between Japan and Russia. The general and his son sent reports back to Washington on the toughness and skill of the Japanese soldiers. They conferred with various leaders. Ceylon (now Sri Lanka), India, Java, Siam (now Thailand) and what is now Vietnam were on their trip of almost twenty thousand miles.

That trip impressed the younger MacArthur with the size and meaning of Asia's huge and changing population, an impression that would never leave him. Out of Asia, he always believed, would come winds of change that would be felt in America and all over the world. "It was crystal clear to me " MacArthur later wrote, "that the future and, indeed, the very existence of America, was irrevocably entwined with Asia and its island outposts." The Orient had cast what he later called "its mystic hold upon me."

Returning to the United States, the son of the famous general was named an aide to the President of the United States, Theodore Roosevelt. At glittering White House parties, Captain Douglas MacArthur chatted with the nation's Senators, cabinet members, diplomats, generals and politicians.

His father had retired from the Army in 1909. He and his wife lived in his hometown of Milwaukee. There, in early September of 1912, the one-time Boy Lieutenant was asked to address the survivors of the 24th Wisconsin at its fiftieth reunion. While speaking to his old comrades, Arthur MacArthur fell to the ground for the last time, dead of a heart attack.

But his father's fame would continue to help Douglas MacArthur. One of his father's comrades on the frontier had been Leonard Wood, now a general and the Army's "boss"—its Chief of Staff. In 1913 Wood appointed thirty-two-year-old MacArthur to the Army's elite General Staff, one of thirty-eight officers who were called "the brains of the Army." It was the job of the General Staff to plan strategy for any future war.

Early in 1914 the dictator, Victoriano Huerta, began to mass troops along the Rio Grande River. In retaliation, President Woodrow Wilson ordered the American Navy to seize the Mexican port of Veracruz. In Washington General Wood began to organize an army to invade Mexico. The army, he decided, would land in Veracruz.

One day he called MacArthur to his office. "Go to Veracruz," he ordered in his brisk way, "and study the lay of the land. How soon can you leave?"

"I'll be off within an hour."

MacArthur rushed back to the apartment he shared with his mother, said a quick good-bye, and the next morning sailed on the battleship *Nebraska*. A week later he prowled the humid, smelly back alleys of Veracruz, seeking information. He knew that General Wood's army would need trains to roll inland from Veracruz. MacArthur wanted to find locomotives to pull those trains. He met a Mexican engineer who agreed, for a hundred and fifty dollars, to take him behind the lines of the Mexican army and show him where a number of locomotives were hidden.

On a dark, stormy night, without informing his superiors in Veracruz of the mission, MacArthur crossed the American lines, wearing his uniform and a revolver on his hip. He met the engineer at the rendezvous and searched him. He took from the man a .38 revolver and a small knife.

"Now you search me," MacArthur told the engineer. He wanted the engineer to see that he carried no money. Killing MacArthur, he wanted the engineer to realize, would do him no good. To be paid, the engineer had to return MacArthur safely to Veracruz.

MacArthur and the engineer, with two other Mexicans, climbed aboard a flat-topped, open railroad handcar and sped forty miles through the night to Alvarado, where they found the locomotives. MacArthur inspected them and concluded that three were "just what we needed—fine big road pullers in excellent condition."

He and his companions started back on the tracks toward

31

Veracruz. MacArthur thought they might have been spotted on their way to Alvarado. Biting his lips, he wondered if Mexican troops might be waiting at the stations of the towns they had to pass through. Just before they reached each town, MacArthur and one Mexican got off the handcar, skirted the town and rejoined the handcar when it had passed through the town.

While MacArthur and his guide stumbled on a dirt road around one town, lashed together so they wouldn't lose each other in the blackness, five armed bandits suddenly loomed in front of them. MacArthur and the Mexican ran. The bandits fired bullets that whined over MacArthur's head. He turned and saw two bandits running toward him. MacArthur jerked out his gun and fired. Both men fell.

MacArthur and the guide ran toward the railroad tracks. If the shots had frightened away the Mexicans on the handcar, he would be trapped behind the Mexican lines. When daylight dawned he would immediately be caught in his American uniform.

They arrived at the tracks. No handcar. They ran along the ties peering into the darkness. Still no handcar. They ran for amost a mile. Puffing hard, MacArthur feared it had gone. But a few minutes later he found it. The Mexicans had raced off after hearing the shots, then stopped to wait for MacArthur. But if he hadn't come in another minute, they would have gone and left him to be caught and probably killed.

The car rushed on toward Veracruz. But at Piedra, as MacArthur and his guide circled the town in a heavy mist, a dozen horsemen suddenly ringed them. One horseman rushed at MacArthur, knocking him off the road into a ditch. A shot rang out and MacArthur saw his guide topple to the ground.

MacArthur jerked out his revolver. It roared four, five, six times in his hand. Four bandits toppled off their horses. MacArthur pulled his bleeding guide to his feet. Together they stumbled through the mist to the tracks where, fortunately, the handcar waited. The car rocketed away while MacArthur patched up the man's wound, which was not serious.

Later, three horsemen suddenly sprinted alongside the handcar and began to fire at it. MacArthur and the Mexicans dropped to the wooden floor. MacArthur fired and two horsemen swerved away. But the third, on a good mount, blasted shots at the handcar. One bullet sang through MacArthur's billowing shirt and two kicked up splinters within six inches of his chest.

MacArthur raised himself on one elbow, aimed carefully, and fired. The bandit flew out of the saddle. MacArthur's grinning companions stood and patted him on the back.

The car came to a narrow, swift-flowing river. The bridge had been knocked down. MacArthur and the Mexicans abandoned the handcar and found the boat they had left to row across the river. But the boat struck a rock and sank quickly. MacArthur grabbed the wounded man and held him afloat. To his relief, MacArthur's feet struck bottom and he waded ashore. If the water had been deeper, all might have drowned, MacArthur said later, "for in our exhausted physical condition I do not believe we would have been capable of swimming."

An hour later the party crossed the American lines. From Veracruz MacArthur cabled General Wood in Washington that his army could roll inland. However, following an apology by the Mexican government for its aggressive acts, the Americans withdrew from Veracruz and the incident ended.

MacArthur's superiors in Veracruz wrote to General Wood and recommended that the young captain receive the Congressional Medal of Honor for his daring adventure. Wood agreed that "services performed clearly entitle him to a Medal of Honor."

A three-man board considered MacArthur for the medal. The board said no. It praised MacArthur for his boldness but noted that he had not informed his superiors of his mission. Giving him the Medal of Honor, the board said, might encourage soldiers or officers to go on adventures fatal to themselves or their units.

MacArthur grumbled his disappointment to his doting mother. He and his father would have been the first father and son to win this highest of all honors. Probably at his mother's urging, MacArthur dashed off a letter to then Army Chief of Staff General Hugh L. Scott protesting the board's decision.

Many generals were aghast at the young captain's boldness—what they called "impertinence." The board's decision stood: MacArthur did not get the medal.

But now he was being watched closely by many of the Army's generals. Douglas MacArthur had become more than the son of the famous hero. Whether or not you liked the ambitious captain and his equally ambitious mother, the Army's generals told one another, you had to agree this MacArthur was intelligent and brave.

Within the next few years, on battlefields in France, he would prove just how brave and intelligent he was.

4

"Over the Country Like a Rainbow"

Silver-haired Newton Baker, Secretary of War, peered over his spectacles at the two officers as they sat down facing his desk. One was the calm and professional-looking General William Mann. The other was the slim, thirty-seven-year-old Major Douglas MacArthur.

"The problem is this, gentlemen," Secretary Baker said after a few brief pleasantries, "if we send to France the New York National Guard troops, some people in New York might say, 'Why send our boys first?' And people in Ohio or California might say we are preferring New York and giving New York the first chance for glory."

MacArthur nodded. Then he said he had an idea. Go ahead, said Secretary Baker impatiently, tell us what it is.

The time was early April, 1917. For the past three years the guns of World War I had roared across Europe as the Allied forces of Britain, France, Italy and Russia battled against Germany and its Central European partners. Early in 1917, after a German U-boat torpedoed an American ship and killed a number of American passengers, Congress, on the urging of President Woodrow Wilson, declared war on Germany. The United States was now assembling an army to fight in France alongside the British and French.

In Europe men were "crafted" into the army. Either they fought or they went to prison. Most Americans had believed that men should volunteer to fight. Americans, many politicians said, would refuse to be drafted.

But MacArthur thought an America at war would accept a draft. As a member of the Army General Staff, he had long conversations with newspaper correspondents in Washington. MacArthur convinced many of the reporters that a draft was the only way to build up America's weak army of a hundred thousand. Many of the reporters wrote stories favoring a draft and persuaded their readers that it was a good idea. In May, 1917, the U.S. Congress passed a "selective service" draft law. Soon hundreds of thousands of drafted men flowed into Army camps. One Army colonel later said: "Make no mistake: It was then-Major Douglas MacArthur . . . who sold the American people the Selective Service Act. . . ."

Now, sitting in Baker's office, MacArthur was answering the secretary's question: Which state's troops should be the first to sail for France? MacArthur pointed out that many states now had too many troops. Why not, he said, take these extra men—say from Ohio or New York or Alabama or California—and form them into a new division? It would be made up of men from nearly all of the states. And this division would be among the first to sail for France.

Baker and General Mann liked the idea. They began to tick off the names of the states that could send troops for this new division.

"Great," said MacArthur. "It would stretch over the country like a rainbow."

And so the most famous American division of the war got its name . . . the Rainbow Division. Officially the 42nd Division, its shoulder patch was a bright rainbow.

Its first commander was the cool, urbane General Mann. Secretary Baker appointed MacArthur as the Rainbow's chief of staff, or second in command. MacArthur protested: he couldn't be second in command. He was only a major, a rank too low to be a division's chief of staff.

"You are wrong," said a smiling Baker, who had come to admire MacArthur. "You are now promoted to a colonel of engineers."

The Corps of Engineers had been MacArthur's branch of service since West Point. But knowing that glory in war is won where his father had won it—with the infantry's foot soldiers—MacArthur asked, "Please make me a colonel of infantry."

"And that is how," he later wrote, "I became a doughboy."

With some twenty thousand other doughboys, as the American infantrymen of World War I were called, MacArthur began training with the Rainbow Division at a Long Island camp. Former plumbers, farmers, carpenters and cooks bumbled and stumbled as they learned how to march and shoot. One regiment, headed to the parade grounds, swung left instead of right, marched out of the camp and got lost on a back road, much to their chief of staff's anger and dismay.

From France, where the American Expeditionary Force's commander, the stiff-mannered General John (Black Jack) Pershing, had set up his headquarters, came insistent pleas: Send American troops! A new German offensive against exhausted Allied troops was expected. When, asked the outnumbered British and French, were the Yanks coming over?

MacArthur knew the Rainbow Division was not ready to fight. But he agreed with General Mann: the 42nd would have to learn under fire. On October 18, 1917, as dockside bands played *"We're coming over ... we're coming over .... the Yanks are coming ..."* the Rainbow soldiers sailed from Hoboken, New Jersey, bound for France.

There MacArthur took the wire ring out of his cap, giving it a floppy rakish look. He never wore a helmet although he ordered all his troops to wear one. "Under fire I haven't got time to change my headgear," he explained not very convincingly. He wore a four-yard-long muffler wrapped around his neck, high-necked sweaters, riding breeches and polished riding boots. Jutting from his mouth was a long jeweled cigarette holder and a riding crop dangled from his wrist. His troops called him "the Fighting Dude."

As chief of staff he worked eighteen hours a day, conferring with General Mann, then snapping out orders to the division's commanders. But from his first day in France he was anxious to prowl the battlefield.

"I cannot fight them," MacArthur pleaded with a French general, "if I cannot see them." He got the general's permission to accompany a French patrol during a night attack.

Near midnight he leaped out of a trench and squirmed along the mucky, barbed-wired, dark landscape of no-man's-land. He crawled behind a cutter who snapped the barbed-wire entanglements. From afar, through the darkness, he heard the clatter and mutter of small-arms fire.

A German sentry spotted them. Bullets whizzed around MacArthur's head. The white lights of German flares lit up the night with a sudden glare. MacArthur hugged the ground, face down. Shells shook the earth around him.

The leader of the trapped patrol decided to rush forward into a German dugout. If they captured the dugout, they would have cover from the iron shrapnel raining down on them. With a shout the French soldiers, MacArthur in their midst, bolted toward the dugout. "The fight was savage and merciless," MacArthur later wrote. "Finally a grenade, tossed into the dugout . . . ended it."

When the shelling ceased, the patrol scuttled back across the dark no-man's-land with several prisoners. After sliding into their trenches, the French soldiers clapped MacArthur on the shoulders and pulled out bottles of absinthe and cognac to share with their new comrade.

A few hours later a French general pinned one of France's highest medals, the Croix de Guerre, on MacArthur. He was the first member of the American Expeditionary Force to receive the medal. Later he was given the American Silver Star for that patrol.

In later years MacArthur often said that "God led me by the hand" across the battlefields of France. "There were so many times," he said with wonder, "I shouldn't have escaped."

Once he organized a night patrol of Rainbow Division soldiers and led them into no-man's-land. After crawling only a few hundred feet through the barbed wire, they were pinned to the ground by waves of machine-gun fire, then by the earth-shattering blasts of mortar shells. Face inches from the mud, he called out into the blackness, "Each one of you get up when I give the signal and take the hand of the man on his right. I will lead off to get back to our lines."

MacArthur gave the command to get up. He heard no scuffling of feet. He gave the command a second time. Still no sounds of men moving. As the shelling diminished, he rose warily and crawled around in the darkness to find his men. He found them all. They were dead.

Once, after a night attack, he fell asleep on the ground with some of his troops. Just before daybreak, for no reason he could later explain, he suddenly awoke. What he saw in front of him—no more than a few hundred yards away—was an entire German regiment, fully armed, marching directly across a nearby road.

MacArthur jabbed the arm of a soldier, awoke him, and whispered, "Do you see what I see?"

The man stared and nodded. MacArthur was relieved; at first he had thought he was seeing men who weren't there. MacArthur then realized what had happened: In the night his soldiers had penetrated deeper into the German lines than the Germans knew.

MacArthur moved along his soldiers, awakening them, "German regiment! German regiment!"

Quickly the machine guns and rifles of the Rainbow's soldiers were pointed at the marching column of Germans in their field-gray uniforms. MacArthur gave the order: "Fire!" Hundreds of the Germans were mowed down and the rest fled in terror.

On another occasion, visiting the front line, MacArthur saw a major give the order for his Rainbow troops to climb out of their trenches—"go over the top," as the saying went—and charge the enemy. His troops, who hated the major, didn't move.

MacArthur knew that these troops had to charge. If they didn't, the advancing Rainbow soldiers on their left and right could be cut down by enemy cross fire.

"I'll take command," MacArthur told the major. He hoped that these Rainbow troops, having seen him so often in the trenches, would trust him with their lives.

As bullets and shells whined overhead, MacArthur walked to the middle of the trench and shouted, "Follow me!"

He leaped to the top of the trench. For a moment he hesitated, then stood and marched into the smoke, flame and thunder of no-man's-land. He did not look back to see if the soldiers were following him. But he had gone only a few steps, "which seemed to me like a hundred," when he heard a shout behind him. Over the top came the rest of the Rainbow troops.

Occasionally MacArthur fought his American superiors with the same intensity he fought the Germans. On the eve of an attack, Colonel MacArthur got an order from General Pershing's headquarters in Chaumont, France, that took away his best officers.

Enraged, MacArthur jumped into his car and sped to Chaumont. He dashed past sentries, flung open the door of Pershing's office, and stared at the tough old Black Jack "with blood in my eye."

He walked up to Pershing's desk and pounded on it. "I can fight the Boches," he shouted, "but I can't fight Chaumont."

"Why Douglas," asked the startled Pershing, "what's the matter?"

MacArthur explained. Pershing countermanded the order. MacArthur went back to his staff and the next day watched his men capture a hill.

But on another occasion he caught the full blast of Black Jack's scalding anger. While driving through a town Pershing saw some of the Rainbow's doughboys who had, only hours before, clambered out of muddy trenches. Pershing glared at their dirty uniforms and unshaven faces.

He saw MacArthur. "MacArthur," he snapped as Rainbow officers and men stared, "the whole outfit is just about the worst I have ever seen. You are personally responsible. It's a disgrace."

He stalked off. An embarrassed MacArthur slumped onto a bench, his face pale. His shoulders sagged with disappointment. Other officers tried to console him, "That's Black Jack's way," one said, "all bluster and fury, but he means only half what he says."

MacArthur was disconsolate. Later he told friends that he knew what the trouble was: "The Chaumont Group," the officers around Black Jack at his headquarters, hated him because they were jealous of his dashing manner and front-line combat record. They were out to get him, he told himself.

And so began MacArthur's feeling that he was being persecuted by envious officers. One of "the Chaumont Group" was a crisply dressed, blue-eyed colonel just about MacArthur's age. His name was George Catlett Marshall. In another war George Marshall would become in MacArthur's mind one of "my enemies behind me."

Pershing was annoyed by MacArthur's impetuousness. Once he told MacArthur, "Young man, I do not like your attitude." But only a few days after he had scolded MacArthur in front of his troops, he promoted him to the one-star rank of brigadier general. MacArthur's mother, who had known Black Jack when he was an officer under her husband, had written to Pershing and begged that he promote her son.

Pershing had other reasons to promote MacArthur, however. "MacArthur," he once said, "is the greatest leader of troops we have." And Pershing also knew that his boss, Secretary of War Baker, admired MacArthur.

41

In any case, at only thirty-eight, MacArthur had become the AEF's youngest general. As they rode to work in their trolley cars or Model A Fords, straw-hatted Americans read newspaper stories from France of this dashing general. War correspondents likened him to one of Alexandre Dumas' fictional Musketeers and called him "the D'Artagnan of the Western Front." Others wrote of his fancy attire and said he was the Beau Brummell of the AEF. He had become one of America's most romantic doughboys. But at a place called Champagne-Marne the new general would become agonizingly aware—perhaps for the first time—just how little of romance there is in war.

5

"Take the Côte-de-Châtillon"

The German prisoner stared sullenly at the French officer who was questioning him. Then, each word dragged slowly out of him, the German told the French officer what the officer had demanded to know: that the big German offensive would start at midnight.

The date was July 14, 1918. A huge German army had formed for a massive blow aimed at Paris. In their muddy, rat-infested trenches the doughboys of the 42nd Rainbow cleaned their rifles, loaded their ammunition belts, oiled their machine guns. That afternoon, alerted by the French, the 42nd's chief of staff, Brigadier General Douglas MacArthur, walked through the trenches to tell his officers and soldiers that the German blow would fall on them at midnight. It would be called the battle of the Champagne-Marne.

"MacArthur is the bloodiest fighting man in this army," the 42nd Division's new commanding general, Charles T. Menoher, remarked once. "I'm afraid we're going to lose him sometime, for there's no risk of battle that any soldier is called upon to take that he is not liable to look up and see MacArthur at his side."

Some officers sneered at "the Dude," as they called him. An inspecting officer from Pershing's headquarters at Chaumont criticized him in a report for not wearing a helmet or a gas mask and for going to the front. MacArthur growled that "the Chaumont Group" was jealous of him because of the American newspaper articles that were appearing about "the D'Artagnan of the Western Front." In his official reply to the report, MacArthur wrote: "I wear no iron helmet because it hurts my head. I carry no gas mask because it hampers my movements. I go unarmed because it is not my purpose to engage in personal combat, but to direct others."

When Pershing's aides read MacArthur's explanation, they scoffed. But Pershing—whatever his personal feelings about MacArthur's sometimes too-bold manner—admired his courage and leadership. He ordered the critical report to be torn up.

On the night before the battle of the Champagne-Marne, MacArthur crouched in a dugout atop a small hill. Just before midnight the British, French and American guns belched shells at the massed German army. The explosions lit up the torn and desolate landscape. At midnight the German guns roared back. "France," wrote one American war correspondent, "was again in peril."

Gripping binoculars, MacArthur watched the Germans swarm across no-man's-land, their figures illuminated as exploding shells crashed around them. He shouted orders to his gunners, telling them where to fire.

For four days the Germans swarmed before the Allied lines and were thrown back, leaving behind thousands of mangled corpses.

"The Germans' last great attack of the war had failed," MacArthur wrote after that Champagne-Marne battle, for which he was awarded a second Silver Star. "And Paris could breathe again."

A few nights later MacArthur and his staff celebrated the victory at a bar in the nearby town of Châlons. Glasses were hoisted high. The Americans sang "Mademoiselle of Armentiers" to the laughing, pink-cheeked barmaids. But often the young general's face turned grim. More than five hundred of his Rainbow soldiers had died stopping the Germans and there was, he later wrote, "the stench of dead flesh still in my nostrils. Perhaps I was just getting old; somehow, I had just forgotten how to play." One MacArthur biographer commented, "War had lost its romance" for the son of the Boy Lieutenant.

The Allies came out of the trenches to attack the exhausted and decimated German army. The Rainbow Division was shipped to an area called Château-Thierry.

To his delight, MacArthur was promoted from division chief of staff to the command of one of the Rainbow's two brigades—the 84th Infantry. The job was the front-line command he had wanted since his arrival in France.

At Château-Thierry MacArthur lived in a ramshackle, mud-floored dugout just behind the front lines. From there he issued orders to the Rainbow's 84th Infantry as it fought what MacArthur later called "six of the bitterest days and nights of the war."

In twos and threes the Rainbow soldiers crept under barbed wire toward chattering German machine guns. They ringed enemy trenches, hurled in grenades, then leaped into the trenches and jabbed bayonets. Step by bloody step the Rainbow drove the Germans back across the Ourcq River, then charged up a steep hill to wipe out an entrenched garrison.

MacArthur had not slept in four days and nights. As he walked to his outposts a quarter of a mile from the enemy lines, he heard across no-man's-land explosions and the coughing of trucks. The Germans, he guessed, were blowing up supplies and withdrawing. If they were, it would be the ideal time to attack.

There was no time to notify the Rainbow Division commander. He had to strike quickly while the enemy was not expecting an attack. But if the attack were repulsed, MacArthur knew he probably would be court-martialed for attacking without orders.

As he later recalled, he made a quick decision. "Advance with audacity," he ordered the 84th Brigade's battalions. They moved out along a line three miles in length.

45

MacArthur himself led an advancing battalion, armed with a pistol, the floppy cap on his head, the flowing scarf wrapped around his throat, the polished boots caked with mud. Next to MacArthur walked a guide carrying a rifle and a string of grenades.

In the blackness there was a suffocating, sickening stench. MacArthur stumbled over corpses and heard the moans and cries of dying Germans. MacArthur estimated later that he passed at least two thousand bodies.

Occasionally a rifle or pistol barked and a shot hummed over their heads. Then, suddenly, a white flare soared across the sky and illuminated the slope they had been climbing. MacArthur and the guide dropped to the ground.

They saw, directly ahead of them, the glittering barrel of a machine gun. Standing over the gun was a German, pointing at them with his extended arm. Two soldiers were hunched over the gun, one aiming, while the other gripped a belt of cartridges.

MacArthur dug his face into the ground, expecting to hear the gun explode a stream of shells. He heard nothing. Cautiously he lifted his head. The flare's light had faded; again there was blackness.

MacArthur and the guide crawled warily across the ground, their guns ready. The guide flicked on a flashlight and—in its pencil of white light—there they stood: the machine-gun crew, one still pointing, the other two hunched over the gun.

"They were never to move," MacArthur wrote. "They were dead . . . the lieutenant with shrapnel through his heart, the sergeant with his belly blown into his back, the corporal with his spine where his head should have been."

MacArthur's Rainbow troops drove the Germans ahead of them. "Advancing my whole line with utmost speed," he reported by radio to headquarters. "I intend to throw the enemy into the Vesle." The Vesle was a river some twenty miles ahead.

The Allies did. For his bold attack MacArthur was given another Silver Star—his fourth. And the French named him a Commander of the Legion of Honor. Back home the "D'Artagnan of the Western Front" had become, next to Pershing, America's most famous general.

But the Rainbow had paid a dreadful price for its victories at Champagne-Marne, the Ourcq, and beyond. In two weeks some sixty-five hundred Rainbow soldiers of the twenty-six thousand men in the division had been killed, wounded or were missing. Pershing ordered the shattered Rainbow to the rear.

"Back came our decimated battalions along the way they had already traveled," the 42nd Division's chaplain, Father Francis Duffy, later wrote. "They marched in wearied silence until they came to the slopes around Meurcy Farm. Then from end to end of the line came the sound of dry, suppressed sobs. They were marching among the bodies of their unburied dead."

By late September, 1918, the Rainbow, strengthened by fresh troops from America (more than one million American soldiers were now in France), stood in the front-line trenches of the Argonne Forest. In four days of fighting in what MacArthur called "this red inferno," one Rainbow brigade had five hundred twenty-eight killed or wounded.

One morning MacArthur crept to the top of a hill to survey the German lines. As he talked to several officers, they were caught in a bombardment of poison-gas shells. Choking, eyes blinded by tears, gasping, they fled down the hill. The next day MacArthur was again caught in another blinding gas attack. He coughed and vomited continually. His staff insisted he go to a hospital, but MacArthur refused. Later he would be awarded two Purple Hearts.

By October 14 the American thrust through the Argonne had been stopped. Holding up the advance was a line of forts centered around several hills called the Côte-de-Châtillon. Pershing ordered the Côte-de-Châtillon to be taken by MacArthur's 84th Infantry Brigade.

An attack was set for dawn of October 14. A few hours before the attack MacArthur was seated at a table in a muddy dugout not far from the lines when Major General Charles Summerall, his Corps commander, walked in and said grimly, "Give me Châtillon, or a list of five thousand casualties."

MacArthur stared at the Corps commander. "All right, General," he said, "we'll take it, or my name will head the list."

General Summerall nodded, and walked out of the dugout into the foggy night. He had every reason to think that he would next see MacArthur dead.

6

"The Loneliest Man I Have Ever Known"

As the tall, broad-shouldered General Summerall shut the door of the dugout, MacArthur reached into the breast pocket of his leather jacket. He took out a silver cigarette case and snapped it open. On the inside was engraved: "To the bravest of the brave." It had been given to him by his staff when he had left the job as Rainbow chief of staff to command the 84th Brigade.

He lit a cigarette, blew out smoke thoughtfully, then began to examine a large photograph spread out on the table.

At MacArthur's orders, the photo had been taken that afternoon by a scout plane. It showed the Côte-de-Châtillon fortifications. As MacArthur had suspected, its barbed wire entanglements were thickest in the center, strung out thinly on the left and right flanks. MacArthur had learned that German generals tended to bunch most of their strength in the middle of their lines.

Picking up a field telephone, MacArthur summoned the commanders of the 84th Brigade, which was made up mostly of Alabamans and Iowans. He told them to concentrate their artillery shells on the thin enemy flanks. "There was where I planned to strike," he reminisced, "with my Alabama cotton-growers on the left, my Iowa farmers on the right."

49

The dawn of October 14 was "dark, misty and forbidding," one Rainbow lieutenant later recalled. Men groaned as they arose—some for the last time—from what the lieutenant called "their beds in the mud."

All during that day MacArthur's Alabamans and Iowans stormed the two key hills of the Côte-de-Châtillon—Hill 288 and Hill 282, both about nine hundred feet high. The Iowa troops swept over Hill 288, killing most of the two thousand Germans atop it, but by nightfall the Germans still were on what MacArthur called "the frowning height of Hill 282."

Again MacArthur conferred with his commanders. A staff officer suggested a plan: a sneak attack through the thin barbed wire on the left and right, the attackers edging as close to the sides of the hill as possible. Then there would be a massive frontal charge as the attackers on the flanks trapped the Germans in a cross fire.

MacArthur liked the idea. The next evening, as dusk fell on the ravaged countryside, the Iowans sneaked through the loosely drawn barbed wire on the flanks. Then, signalled by the shrill blasts of whistles, the Alabamans rushed directly into the blazing fire of the Germans atop the hill. "Officers fell and sergeants leaped to the command," MacArthur later recalled. "Companies dwindled to platoons and corporals took over."

MacArthur rallied the charging Alabama troops when they wavered. He joined the cheers when they heard the crashing sounds of the cross fire coming from the Iowans onto the surprised German flanks. One soldier, Private Thomas C. Neibaur, crawled up the hill with two broken legs, firing as he crawled, and at the top he captured eleven Germans. He would be awarded the Congressional Medal of Honor.

At the top of Hill 282 the Iowans and Alabamans came together over the strewn bodies of Germans. At six p.m., as blackness fell over Hill 282, MacArthur proudly called General Summerall to report, "The Côte-de-Châtillon has fallen."

But at a price. Only three hundred men and six officers stood of the thousand four hundred fifty men and twenty-five officers of the Iowa battalion. The two-day siege had cost four thousand killed or wounded. In later years, said MacArthur's biographer Frazier Hunt, the general "could never even mention the name Côte-de-Châtillon without visible emotion."

General Summerall recommended that MacArthur be awarded the Congressional Medal of Honor for his "indomitable resolution and great courage in rallying broken lines. . . ." But for the second time in six years that medal, won by his father, was denied MacArthur. Pershing's headquarters turned down Summerall's nomination. Again MacArthur was consumed by the feeling that "people around Pershing," such as Colonel George C. Marshall, did not like him and were envious of him.

MacArthur was awarded the Distinguished Service Cross. Later Pershing declared that Côte-de-Châtillon was the "decisive blow" that ended the war. As the shattered, weary German army retreated toward Germany, MacArthur took command of the Rainbow Division (General Menoher had been promoted to commander of a corps). A month after the Rainbow's victory at Côte-de-Châtillon, the war ended. An armistice was signed on November 11, 1918, and victorious Allied troops poured into defeated Germany.

For six months the Rainbow patrolled the green countryside along the Rhine River. MacArthur lived in a palatial stone mansion overlooking the winding river. For the Rainbow soldiers the time was a well-earned rest. In a hundred sixty-two days of muderous combat almost one of every two Rainbow soldiers had been killed or wounded—a total of fourteen thousand six hundred eighty-three casualties, two thousand seven hundred thirteen dead.

Brigadier General MacArthur had come out of the war as one of America's most decorated fighting men. On his chest he wore two DSC's, seven Silver Stars, two Purple Hearts, and several French and other foreign medals. Most Americans agreed with Secretary

51

Baker's appraisal of MacArthur as "the greatest front-line general" of the war.

In April, of 1919, the Rainbow Division sailed for home. By then the war was half forgotten in America. When MacArthur, attired in a raccoon coat and his floppy hat, strode down the gangplank in New York, he was stopped by a small boy, who asked: "What division is this?"

"We are the famous 42nd," said MacArthur proudly.

"Oh," said the boy, "and was this division in France?"

"Amid a silence that hurt," MacArthur later said, ". . . we marched off the dock, to be scattered to the four winds—a sad, gloomy end of the Rainbow."

His soldiers went back to their civilian lives as street car conductors, plumbers, mechanics, cotton growers and farmers. MacArthur would be going back to West Point.

He strode into the office of the white-haired General Peyton March, the Army Chief of Staff, and saluted. General March snapped back a salute, then smiled and shook MacArthur's hand. General March had been a lieutenant in the Philippines under General Arthur MacArthur. Now, as they faced each other across General March's desk, the Chief of Staff gave the general's son his first postwar assignment. "General," said the smiling March, "I want you to be the new superintendent of West Point."

MacArthur was startled. "I am not an educator, I am a field soldier," he told March. Also he was only thirty-nine years old on this spring day in 1919; the previous superintendent of West Point had been seventy-one. "Besides," he added, "there are so many of my old professors there." How could he be their boss?

But March was adamant. MacArthur went to West Point, the youngest superintendent of the Academy since its founding father, Sylvanus Thayer, back in 1813. His mother, as she had some twenty-five years earlier, accompanied him. This time they lived together in the superintendent's rambling stone mansion.

In his first few weeks at West Point MacArthur realized that the Academy was old-fashioned. Professors taught classes as they had been taught in the Nineteenth Century. MacArthur saw cadets marching erectly on sentry duty and said, "In France, if they had marched sentry duty like that, they wouldn't have lasted a minute before their heads were blown off." And to an assistant he remarked, "How long are we going on preparing the cadets for the War of 1812?"

MacArthur threw open the windows of West Point to bring in the fresh breezes of the Twentieth Century. He made the strict life of the cadets much freer. "We give the lowliest Army private weekend passes," he told aides. "Is a cadet at least not as honorable and trustworthy? He shouldn't be treated like a prisoner."

He ordered modern textbooks and new teaching methods for the classrooms. One of MacArthur's aides warned him that the professors would oppose the new ideas. MacArthur laughed. "We met more than that in France," he said, "and won."

And in the years from 1919 to 1922 he gave West Point a fresh new look. Cadets walked with a bouncier step, feeling a new pride in themselves. For the first time they were allowed to leave the grounds on weekends. They were given five dollars monthly to spend as they liked. And instead of being shut up in their rooms on Sundays, they could play games on the athletic fields.

To attract more young men to West Point, MacArthur wanted a winning football team. The nation had suddenly become agog over college football—"King Football," as it was called. Each Saturday, in a nation celebrating the end of war, as many as a hundred thousand people jammed college stadiums. Soon the Academy was getting speedy players. The Army team quickly became one of the finest in the nation—a hundred thousand and more watching its annual game against Navy.

MacArthur ordered these words to be engraved over the stone

entrance to the West Point gymnasium: "Upon the fields of friendly strife are sown the seeds that, upon other fields, on other days, will bear the fruits of victory."

One fall afternoon West Point's football team defeated Navy. That night, in defiance of regulations, the cadets celebrated. They streamed out of their stone-walled dormitories to whoop around bonfires.

MacArthur heard the sounds of the celebrating from his home. The next morning he said to one of his staff officers, "Well, that was quite a party last night."

"Yes, sir," said the officer warily, "it was quite a party."

"How many did you skin?" MacArthur asked, meaning how many cadets had been given demerits for being out of quarters.

"Not a one, sir," said the officer nervously.

MacArthur pounded his fist on his desk and shouted, "Good! You know I could hardly resist the impulse to get out and join them."

But MacArthur could be strict when he thought he had to. One day he stared angrily at the student newspaper, *The Brag*, which had printed a humorous article that was critical of him. He ordered that copies of the paper be destroyed. "MacArthur's changes," said a West Point officer of that time, "did not include cadet freedom of the press."

As popular as he was with most of the cadets, however, MacArthur stayed aloof from them and his staff. He disappeared into his large house each night, alone there with his mother and servants. Rarely did he appear at one of the many parties at officers' homes. His wartime friend, correspondent Frazier Hunt, once called him "a lone wolf." And an officer at West Point said he was "one of the loneliest men I have ever known."

He himself told his chief assistant at the Academy: "When a man gets to be a general officer, he has no friends."

More and more he was convinced he had enemies. After the war, as the American Army shrank from two million to about a hundred

54

thousand, many officers were forced to retire. Others were de-moted. Colonel George C. Marshall, for example, had been reduced to a major. But MacArthur, because he had been promoted early in the war, kept his rank of one-star brigadier general. He was sure that officers such as Marshall resented being demoted and were jealous of him.

In 1921 Black Jack Pershing succeeded Peyton March as Chief of Staff. The scowling Black Jack was one of those who grumbled about MacArthur's "new-fangled" changes at West Point. Late in 1921 Black Jack notified MacArthur that he would be replaced as West Point superintendent in June, 1922, and sent to an overseas assignment.

MacArthur was replaced by an older general, who brought back the old and harsh regulations of West Point. But MacArthur had thrown open the windows of that "Monastery on the Hudson." West Point would never be the same. In 1925 a younger superintendent was appointed and he announced, "Every MacArthur change is coming back in full force. His principles and practices will be carried out and improved upon."

"If Sylvanus Thayer was the father of West Point," a member of MacArthur's staff there later declared proudly, "then MacArthur was its savior."

And a MacArthur biographer, D. Clayton James, has written: ". . . there is general agreement that he, more than any other man, led West Point across the threshold into the rapidly changing world of modern military education. . . ."

To many American women of the 1920s Douglas MacArthur—the dashing general and famous war hero—was the most attractive man of the time. A newspaper writer described him as having "the grace and charm of a stage hero . . . I had never before met so vivid, so captivating, so magnetic a man. . . . He stood six feet, had a clean-shaven face, a clean-cut mouth, nose and chin, lots of brown hair, good eyes with a 'come-hither' in them that must have played the devil with the girls."

Hostesses of parties in nearby New York City would have been honored to entertain the distinguished West Point general. But rarely did he attend these parties. He stayed with his mother in their house high above the Hudson. Past seventy by then, Pinky MacArthur had become sickly. Several doctors told MacArthur that she would not live long.

It was a surprise to even his best friends when early in 1922 MacArthur suddenly married Louise Brooks, a beautiful Baltimore society woman whom he'd first known in Paris during World War I. A divorced woman, she had a son and daughter by a previous marriage. They were married at the home of Mrs. Brooks' family— they were very wealthy—in Palm Beach, Florida, on February 14, Valentine's Day.

Tall and dark-eyed Louise Brooks loved the gay social whirl of parties and nightclubs. In Paris during World War I she'd been seen on the arms of numerous American officers, including Black Jack Pershing. Her friends said that in marrying MacArthur she got what she had always wanted—a famous and handsome general.

Leaving West Point, the MacArthurs sailed for the Philippines, MacArthur's new assignment. (His mother, perhaps not caring for her new daughter-in-law, decided to live with her other son, Arthur, now a Navy captain, in Washington.)

As his ship steamed into Manila harbor, MacArthur looked once more at the places he had seen on his first assignment twenty years earlier, the places where his father's invading army had fought and conquered. From the railing of his ship he gazed once more at "the massive bluff of Bataan" and "the lean gray grimness of Corregidor." "It was good to be back . . ." he later wrote, "and to see the progress that had been made."

Many Filipinos wanted their multi-island nation to be independent. One such man was Manuel Quezon, a fiery speaker. He argued that the Philippines should graduate from being a colony to a new status; a semi-independent commonwealth overseen by Washington, then, after a few years, to become an independent nation.

The name MacArthur brought smiles to faces of Filipinos like Quezon. As the first military commander of the Philippines, General Arthur MacArthur had been well-liked. Douglas MacArthur showed his father's human concern and warmth for Filipinos. Unlike other American colonists in Manila, he didn't look down his nose at the brown-skinned "natives." Many Americans spoke insultingly of the poor and uneducated Filipinos as "the white man's burden." To MacArthur, Americans and Filipinos were brothers under one flag—America's.

One morning he learned that an Army ferry boat that shuttled troops and civilians between Manila and Corregidor carried signs forbidding Filipinos to ride on the breezy upper deck. MacArthur immediately phoned the commanding officer at Corregidor to ask why the Filipinos were forbidden to ride on the upper deck.

"But the regulations are clear," the officer stammered.

"You change them at once!" MacArthur snapped. "Understand, at once!"

The MacArthurs entertained Mr. and Mrs. Quezon and other Filipino couples at their home—to the disapproval of many Americans in Manila. Ignoring them, MacArthur soon made Quezon his closest friend in the Philippines. The two often talked until late at night about the future of the country and its people. In a way, the Philippines soon became MacArthur's adopted country.

MacArthur and his wife returned briefly to the United States in 1923, because of a serious ailment of his mother, who recovered. Later that year, however, his brother Arthur suddenly died after an attack of appendicitis. MacArthur arranged for his mother and sister-in-law to live together in Washington, then returned with his wife to his garrison in Manila.

In Washington, though still frail, Pinky MacArthur worked and planned unceasingly for her son's advancement. She had known Black Jack Pershing when he was a lowly lieutenant serving under her husband. She wrote him a flattering letter. She told him he was still "wonderfully handsome" and expressed the hope that one day God would take him "to the White House." She begged the Chief of Staff to promote "my boy" to major general.

Pershing, soon to retire as Chief of Staff, may have been moved by her letter and a loyalty to his dead commanding general. For whatever reason, just ten days before Pershing retired as Chief of Staff, MacArthur's prospective promotion to the rank of major general was announced. On January 17, 1925, he became the youngest two-star general in the Army.

At the age of only forty-four MacArthur still had some twenty years of Army service ahead of him. Almost certainly, before he retired he would be the Army's boss—the four-star Chief of Staff.

In 1925 the MacArthurs returned to the United States. The new major general was put in command of an Army corps whose headquarters were near Baltimore. Louise MacArthur was delighted to be back home in the rolling green hills of Maryland where she had grown up. Riding with her friends, she confessed that Army life in hot and faraway Manila had bored her. She soon was happily sweeping through the social life she loved.

To MacArthur she suggested: Quit the Army. Her rich friends, making millions as the stock market soared, would give him a high-salaried job as a business executive. But MacArthur hated the idea. A man whose grandfather had been a distinguished jurist, he frowned at what was going on in America during those years. Men and women were making fast millions in a stock market gone mad; old moral values had been forgotten by many; the Teapot Dome Scandal had revealed corruption in the highest levels of government, even to the President's Cabinet.

MacArthur and Louise began to drift apart. MacArthur stayed at his Corps headquarters all day and during many evenings while Louise danced at parties. Within a few years they were divorced. She later married a then-famous Hollywood actor, Lionel Atwell. A reporter once asked her what was the difference between being married to the dramatic MacArthur and an actor. She replied, perhaps truthfully: "No difference."

With America on a wild and joyous spree, it seemed the fun and the money making would never end. Many Americans lived in abject poverty. But others danced the Charleston as music blared from their new radios and phonographs; they roared down roads in fast roadsters like the Stutz Bearcat; they drank in illegal speakeasies.

Most Americans ignored the storm clouds building up over Europe and Asia. In Japan the ambitious warlord, General Hideki Tojo, was planning to grab more land for his people bottled up on their crowded islands. In Europe another would-be warlord, Adolf Hitler, screamed to Germans that they needed more land as "breathing room" for their sixty million hungry and restless people.

By the early 1930s the armies of Japan and Germany had swelled—Japan's army to more than a million, Germany's soon to be a million. Well-trained, they rode in tanks and fast new armored cars. Above their heads roared thousands of fighters and bombers. On the other hand, the American Army was only about a hundred thousand strong. It had only a few new tanks and warplanes; many of its troops still rode on horseback and carried World War I rifles.

MacArthur would soon be given the thankless job of trying to build up that army. But first he would go back to the Philippines, where he would say a nervous "no" to the President of the United States.

7

"You Must Not Talk That Way to the President!"

Colonel Eddie Brown tapped lightly on the door of MacArthur's bedroom. He glanced at his watch and saw that the time was a few minutes before five in the morning of a sultry day in Manila late in July, 1929. In his bed MacArthur stirred at the sound of the tapping, then said, "Come in!"

Brown entered the room as MacArthur flicked on a light. A short, cheerful man, Eddie Brown had been one of MacArthur's classmates at West Point. Now he was MacArthur's chief of staff in Manila, where MacArthur commanded U.S. Army forces. He handed MacArthur an envelope stamped: "Secret: For MacArthur's Eyes Only."

MacArthur ripped open the envelope and scanned the lines of a cable from Washington: "The President desires to appoint you as Chief of Engineers . . . . The President desires to know whether you are willing to accept the appointment." The cable was signed by General Charles P. Summerall, MacArthur's old corps commander in France, now Army Chief of Staff.

During the next few days MacArthur pondered what his answer should be, much to Brown's puzzlement. MacArthur paced in front of his desk, a habit he had developed when he was making decisions. "Why don't you say yes?" Brown asked.

MacArthur explained his hesitation. True enough, the post of Chief of Engineers was the second highest in the Army, second only to Chief of Staff. But MacArthur had his reasons not to want the job. One: He had been an infantry officer since 1917 and had not kept up on the new ideas in engineering. Army engineers, MacArthur told Brown, would quickly realize that their boss didn't know as much as they did. Then there was a second reason: No one had ever gone from Chief of Engineers to the No. 1 job, Chief of Staff. And MacArthur wanted that No. 1 job.

"But you can't say no," Brown told him. "The President will be annoyed if you turn him down. You'll never get another promotion. You will have dug your own grave if you refuse."

MacArthur decided to say no. In a delicately worded cable, he suggested to the President that another general would be a better choice as Chief of Engineers. That other general got the job. And in Manila MacArthur sat back to see what the President would do when General Summerall's term as Chief of Staff expired in 1930.

The President was Herbert Hoover, and he had more worrisome concerns than who would be his next Chief of Staff. In the fall of 1929 the stock market collapsed, signaling a coming worldwide economic depression. Millionaires suddenly became paupers. Those who had bought stocks on margin sometimes owed hundreds of thousands of dollars. Some committed suicide.

After the stock market collapse, Americans began to buy fewer goods. Products piled up on shelves, factories got fewer orders to make goods and many shut down. Millions of men and women had no jobs. They walked the streets, desperate, while at home their children were hungry. Soon, as one leader of the time put it, "one-third of the nation was ill-clothed, ill-housed, ill-fed." For Americans the gay party of the Roaring Twenties had ended. Now came the painful days of the Great Depression of the Thirties.

From Manila MacArthur wrote to Pat Hurley, the loud, back-slapping Oklahoma oilman who was President Hoover's Secretary of War and had been a major in France under MacArthur. MacArthur praised Hurley for his "dedication" to his nation. With a bit of flattery similar to his mother's letter to Pershing, MacArthur suggested that one day Hurley might be President of the United States.

Hurley had always liked MacArthur, though he disapproved of his divorce. He began to hint to Hoover that MacArthur succeed Summerall. But Black Jack Pershing, who was a good friend of Hoover's, nominated General Fox Conner, who had been on his Chaumont staff during the war.

Hurley prevailed over Pershing, however. On August 5, 1930, MacArthur received a cable from Washington: "President has just announced your detail as Chief of Staff to succeed General Summerall. . . ."

At fifty he had become one of the youngest Chiefs of Staff in Army history. In the fall of 1930 he boarded a ship bound for San Francisco. Saying good-bye to him was Manuel Quezon, who begged him to return to the Philippines when his term as Chief of Staff expired.

In Washington on November 5 he was sworn in as Chief of Staff, an honor that not even his father, a three-star lieutenant general, had attained. His proud mother pinned the four stars of a full general on his shoulders. Pinky MacArthur, now seventy-eight and very frail, moved with her son into the Army's "Number One Quarters"—the Chief of Staff's large brick home at Fort Myer, Virginia, across the Potomac River from Washington. MacArthur ordered a sun porch to be erected for his mother on the second floor of the house. Then, as he said later, he got ready "to face the music." He was the commander of a puny army in a world of giants.

MacArthur stood in front of the long line of troops. Cavalrymen bobbed on horseback. Next to MacArthur stood a round-faced, broad-shouldered major, Dwight David Eisenhower, whom almost everyone called "Ike."

It was 4:30 in the humid afternoon of July 28, 1932. The troops were massed on Pennsylvania Avenue in Washington, only a few hundred yards from the White House. They gripped rifles and Tommy guns; smoke bombs and hand grenades were clipped to their belts. They faced a raggedly dressed mob of angry, screaming men who called themselves "the Bonus Marchers."

The Bonus Marchers had been World War I soldiers. In the early 1920s the Congress had voted a thousand-dollar bonus to all World War soldiers, to be paid in 1945, when they would be middle-aged or elderly. But many veterans, penniless in the Depression, de- manded the money now to feed themselves and their children. More than twenty thousand had marched into Washington and pitched tents along a muddy swamp near the Anacostia River. Each day, with their wives and children, the Bonus Marchers ringed the White House and clamored for their money.

President Hoover and some Americans—MacArthur was among them—claimed that the Bonus Marchers were led by Communists. The Bonus March, Hoover claimed, was part of a plot by Russia's new Communist leaders to overthrow the U.S. government and make America a Communist state. The Communists, in fact, had been trying to organize unemployed factory workers. Some Com- munist leaders later admitted that they had hoped the Bonus Marchers would attack the Army's soldiers. Blood would be spilled, enraging the nation.

In truth, most historians now believe, there were only a few Communists among the Bonus Marchers. The majority of the marchers were loyal Americans who wanted only their money.

On this July morning the Washington police opened fire. Two marchers were killed. Informed of the killings, Hoover told aides that he feared the infuriated marchers would storm the White House. He ordered MacArthur to clear the streets near the White House of the Bonus Marchers.

MacArthur, with two of his aides, Major Eisenhower and Major George S. Patton, assembled six hundred soldiers, some on horseback. Bayonets fixed to their rifles, the troops faced the several thousand unarmed Bonus Marchers. Thousand of spectators packed the sidewalks.

A whistle shrilled through the heavy heat, and troops began to march toward the veterans. Tear gas bombs burst among the jeering veterans. Tears streamed down their faces as they turned and ran, chased by glistening bayonets and galloping horses. MacArthur, with Eisenhower and Patton at his side, followed on foot as his troops pursued the veterans toward their squalid, patched tents on the Anacostia River mud flats.

Then MacArthur halted his troops, and gave the veterans until midnight to gather up their possessions and leave. Twice that evening President Hoover sent messages to MacArthur, telling him not to drive the veterans from their tents. MacArthur did not obey. He said he was too busy to bother with the orders of "civilians not at the scene."

Near midnight his troops charged into the mud flats. They set fire to the tents. Tongues of orange flames licked high into the night sky over Washington as the veterans, possessions on their backs, fled southward into Virginia. Wives and children stumbled at their sides. Many limped after being butted by rifles. But there were only a few casualties: a seven-year-old boy, who had dashed back to his tent to get a pet rabbit, had been gashed in the leg by a bayonet, and a veteran had an ear lopped off by a cavalryman's saber.

Later that night MacArthur told reporters at the War Department: "That mob down there was a bad-looking mob. It was animated by the essence of revolution. . . ."

The next morning Americans woke to hear on their radios or read in the newspapers about what would become known as the Battle of Anacostia Flats. Some said Hoover and MacArthur had done the right thing. But many others were outraged that American army bayonets had been thrust at men who had fought and bled for their nation in France.

During the next week some Washington reporters, irritated by MacArthur's emperorlike words after the battle, claimed that he had galloped toward the veterans on a white charger, swinging a bloody saber. "There was no fiery white charger," MacArthur replied heatedly and correctly. "There was no saber."

But a new picture had been painted of him—the bloodthirsty, arrogant MacArthur. He would never outlive that portrait. There are still living Americans who think of him as having ruthlessly cut down Bonus Marchers with a swinging saber.

MacArthur began to believe there was a new enemy "out to get me"—the Communists of America and Russia. "It was the beginning," he later wrote, "of a definite and ceaseless campaign that set me apart as a man to be destroyed, no matter how long the Communists . . . had to wait. . . . But it was to be nineteen years before the bells of Moscow pealed out their glee at my eclipse."

During the next few years the Army's Chief of Staff begged the Congress and the President for money to build up the Army and its rickety Air Corps. In Europe, which MacArthur had visited in 1931 and 1932, Hitler would soon be building a war machine for a new kind of war—a blitzkreig, or lightning war, in which the enemy would be annihilated swiftly. In hidden arsenals Germany was collecting the matériel for a huge, fast-moving army. Meanwhile, in Asia the armies of Japan carried their Rising Sun banners into the vastness of China.

Most Americans frowned at news of war. In thousands of homes there were the framed photos of Americans who had been killed in France. "Let's stay out of the rest of the world's battles," many Americans told one another. Called isolationists, they believed America should stay clear of all foreign entanglements.

In 1932 the United States elected a new President, Franklin

Delano Roosevelt. As a young man he had been stricken by poliomyelitis, which paralyzed his legs but did not subdue his spirit. He had to live in a wheelchair. Jaunty in manner, he often had a cigarette holder poking out of his mouth rakishly. He spoke in a clipped, aristocratic way as he tried to pick up the spirits of Depression-weary Americans. In a famous "fireside chat" he told millions of Americans listening on their radios: "The only thing we have to fear is fear itself."

He began a New Deal program to help the poor, who were given coupons to buy food. Men were hired to build new roads, libraries and post offices across the country, their Works Progress Administration wages paid by the government.

Roosevelt's Army Chief of Staff shook his head over many of the New Deal's help-the-poor programs. Like his political idol, ex-President Hoover, MacArthur thought that Americans should lift themselves out of the ditch of poverty; they didn't need any helping hand from the government, he believed. But he kept his ideas to himself, careful not to offend his commander in chief.

He and Roosevelt soon became almost chummy, swapping ideas at White House meetings.

"Why do you listen to me, Mr. President?" MacArthur once asked, "when I am no authority on social reforms?"

"Douglas," said the President, "I don't bring these questions up for your advice but for your reactions. To me, you are the symbol of the conscience of the American people."

Roosevelt was an astute actor who often played roles. What he probably really meant was that Douglas MacArthur was a symbol of conservatives who opposed him; Roosevelt wanted to know their thinking. Like any good general, Roosevelt realized that you must know your enemy to beat him.

Inevitably, these two strong-willed men—both the dramatic-actor type—would clash. That happened one day at the White House as MacArthur argued for more money for the Army. With

66

MacArthur was the lanky Secretary of War George Dern. As they placed arguments in front of Roosevelt, he swept them away with one clever reason after another. Anger began to simmer in MacArthur until he felt nauseous.

Suddenly, as Roosevelt was scornfully laughing at one of Dern's arguments, MacArthur interrupted. His voice shrill, MacArthur shouted, jaw to jaw with the President, that when America lost the next war, an American soldier would be lying in the mud with an enemy bayonet through his stomach. As that soldier "spat out his last curse," MacArthur snapped at the President, he wanted that curse "not to be MacArthur but Roosevelt."

The President gripped hard the sides of his wheelchair, his face pale. "You must not talk that way to the President!" he roared.

MacArthur immediately regretted his insubordinate and insolent words. Rising, he told the President he would resign immediately. He walked toward the door, seeing it as the exit to his military career.

But the President called after him: "Don't be foolish, Douglas. You and the budget must get together on this."

Minutes later, as they stood on the White House steps, Dern clapped a white-faced MacArthur on the back and shouted gleefully, "You've saved the Army!"

MacArthur stared for a moment at Dern, then turned and vomited.

That, at least, is the way MacArthur described what happened.

But Federal funds came only in drops to the Army. By 1935, when his term as Chief of Staff was about to expire (it had been extended a year by Roosevelt), MacArthur had been able to raise the Army's total to only a hundred sixty-five thousand men. And it lacked new tanks and bombers which would be needed in modern war—what MacArthur called "total war," the extermination of cities as well as armies.

At the age of fifty-five MacArthur now faced an embarrassing situation. He would have to step down as the Army's No. 1 commander. But he was ten years away from retirement. How could he take a No. 2 or No. 3 job in the Army during the next ten years, serving under someone else, when he had been No. 1?

One day a bronze-faced visitor, wearing one of the straw-hat "boaters" that were popular during the Thirties, strolled into his office. He was Manuel Quezon, just arrived on a visit from Manila. The Philippines would soon become a semi-independent Commonwealth of the United States and Quezon the Commonwealth's first president.

Facing MacArthur across a desk, Quezon asked: "Do you think the Philippines could be defended against an attack by Japan?"

"If you build up a strong army," MacArthur replied, "no nation will care to attack you, for the cost of conquest will be more than the expected profits."

Quezon then asked: "Would you return to the Philippines as the Commonwealth's military adviser?"

MacArthur said he would consider the offer. He talked it over with his mother, now eighty-four and very ill. Her advice was firm: "I feel it is ordained that you go, and that it will lead you to an even greater role."

Her prophesy would come true. For in Manila MacArthur would play a role greater than anyone could have imagined.

8

"Jap Planes Are Attacking Pearl Harbor"

MacArthur paced the terrace of his penthouse apartment above the streets of Manila, whose lights looked like rows of glittering necklaces.

This was the night of December 7, 1941. For the past five years MacArthur had been the field marshal of the Philippine Army. Much had happened to him and to his career during those five years.

After his arrival in Manila in 1935, and even before he became field marshal, MacArthur began to build up the ragtag Philippine Army. He was aided by his amiable chief of staff, Major Dwight D. Eisenhower. During those years MacArthur built up a Philippine defense force of some hundred thousand Filipinos and twenty-five thousand American Army soldiers and pilots. Another eighty thousand Filipinos had been given military training and could be called up to fight. At nearby Clark Field sat a fleet of new B-17 Flying Fortresses. It was believed that the big bombers—there were thirty-five of them now in the Philippines—could blow any invasion armada out of the ocean.

For the past year Japan and America had stared angrily at each other across the Pacific. President Roosevelt had warned the

Japanese: Stop your thrusts into other Asian countries. Japan had countered that America and European "imperialists" should be thrown out of their colonies in Asia. Japan's war lords planned to bring those countries into a new Japanese empire called the "Greater East Asia Co-Prosperity Sphere."

To grab those colonies, rich with oil and tin and rubber for Japanese factories, Japan had to strike south from its islands. But the Philippine Islands stretched across Japan's path to the south like a dragnet of chains. From the Philippines American ships and planes could block Japan's invasion fleets as they steamed toward the riches of southeast Asia.

Japan's war planners decided to attack America and capture the Philippines. Their plans pleased Adolf Hitler, the Nazi dictator whose Panzer armies had swept through nearly all of Europe during the previous two years. Nazi swastikas now floated from the sandy French beaches along the English Channel to the gateway cities of Asia. Hitler believed that if Japan started war in the Pacific, the United States would not be able to turn to aid England and Russia.

To attack America, Japan's military rulers, led by General Hideki Tojo, devised a timetable. They would dispatch emissaries to Washington to talk of peace, hoping to lull America. Then they would send carriers with aircraft to bomb Pearl Harbor, the Navy's base in Hawaii. That attack, the Japanese hoped, would sink enough battleships so that the Navy could not send help to the Philippines. The Japanese would next overwhelm the cutoff American garrison in the Philippines. With no threat at their backs, the Japanese would then advance into southeast Asia and the Netherlands East Indies.

But America's generals and admirals knew some of Japan's plans. The United States had cracked some Japanese codes. When orders were flashed by radio to the Japanese Navy, American codebreakers could read some of the messages.

In late 1941 the naval eavesdroppers informed the U. S. General Staff that Japan was planning an attack. However, the codebreakers hadn't been able to learn when or where the Japanese would strike. From Washington "war alert" orders were sent to the Army and Navy commanders in Hawaii and to MacArthur in Manila: Be ready for a surprise attack. But it was impossible to predict specifically when the attack would come.

In Manila MacArthur told reporters he expected the attack to be launched in April, 1942. He believed that the Japanese, their armies battling in China, were not yet ready to strike southward—a belief that would soon turn out to be wrong.

When MacArthur came to the Philippines, the American plan to defend the Commonwealth had been this: The Americans and Filipinos would retreat into the largely jungle peninsula of Bataan and onto the nearby rocky island of Corregidor. Based on Bataan and Corregidor, they could block any invader from using Manila to spring toward southeast Asia. According to the American plan—it was called War Plan Orange—the Americans and Filipinos would hold out on Bataan and Corregidor for six months; by then battleships would arrive from Hawaii to lift the siege and chase away the enemy.

MacArthur was contemptuous of the decades-old War Plan Orange, as were most American strategists. MacArthur thought it too defensive. After building up the Philippine army, MacArthur proposed a new plan to General George C. Marshall, the former member of Pershing's Chaumont staff who was now Army Chief of Staff. "We will meet the Japanese on the beaches," his plan said, in effect, "and throw them into the sea." In cables to Marshall, MacArthur emphasized the strength of his growing army. In November, 1941, somewhat reluctantly, Marshall approved the MacArthur plan.

By now MacArthur had given up his post as field marshal of the Philippine defense force and was again a U.S. Army general, commanding both Filipino and U.S. troops. In June, 1941, worried about a Japanese attack, President Roosevelt had called him back

71

into U.S. service, this time with the three-star rank of lieutenant general.

MacArthur, still standing on the terrace of his apartment above Manila on this night of December 7, 1941, glanced at his watch. The time was almost midnight. Inside, waiting for him to retire, was the petite and fair-haired former Jean Marie Faircloth, his wife of four years. In 1937, with MacArthur at her bedside in Manila, Pinky MacArthur had died. His mother's body had been taken to the United States to be buried at Arlington National Cemetery. MacArthur accompanied the body and during the journey he met Jean Faircloth, like his mother, a girl from the American South. MacArthur was immediately entranced by Jean's girlish warmth and charm. She was some twenty years younger than the famous general and looked up at him worshipfully. After a brief courtship, they were married in New York in 1937 before a city clerk, the General dressed in a Homburg hat and a civilian suit. The newlyweds journeyed to Manila. There a son was born in 1938. In honor of the "Boy Lieutenant" who was his grandfather, the child was named Arthur.

A father at fifty-eight MacArthur doted on the baby. He nicknamed him "Sergeant"; right from the start MacArthur had chosen a military career for his son. To the dismay of Jean, MacArthur would pick up and coddle the child whenever he let out a cry. "General," Jean would protest (she nearly always called him "General" in public), "you will spoil the child."

Now, on this night of December 7, MacArthur left the terrace to look in on the baby one last time. Then he retired to his bedroom. At that moment, more than four thousand miles distant across the Pacific, Japanese planes were lifting off the decks of aircraft carriers to drone toward Pearl Harbor. Moving with radios silent, a Japanese task force had crept within striking distance of the anchored Pacific Fleet. And by not sending or receiving radio messages, the task force had not been detected by America's codebreakers.

The phone rang shrilly in the darkness of the bedroom. The time was 3:40 in the morning of December 8, Manila time, about noon of December 7 in America. MacArthur reached across the bed and picked up the phone. Calling was his chief of staff, Colonel Dick Sutherland.*

"Jap planes are attacking Pearl Harbor," Sutherland snapped coolly.

"Pearl Harbor!" MacArthur's voice showed his surprise. "That should be our strongest point!"

He didn't yet know that the Japanese bombers had surprised the Navy on a serene Sunday morning in Pearl Harbor. The Navy's big battlewagons had been tied up in rows, sitting ducks for the Japanese bombs. Right now, with hundreds of sailors dead, the Pacific Fleet's biggest battleships were flaming wrecks. The back of the fleet had been broken.

MacArthur dressed quickly, donning his starched suntan uniform, three stars on his open collar. He put on his floppy cap with the gold "scrambled eggs" embroidery on the stiff visor and rode in his black 1941 Cadillac through the dark streets of Manila to his headquarters, a clump of squat buildings near the city's old walled quarter, the Intramuros. Awaiting him were Sutherland and other officers. As soon as MacArthur sat down, they ringed his desk and began to confer.

A few minutes earlier General Lewis Brereton, the commander of MacArthur's air corps, had phoned Sutherland. He had begged Sutherland to allow him to unleash some of his B-17 bombers at the Japanese air base on Formosa, some five hundred miles to the north. Sutherland scotched the idea. Brereton asked to talk to MacArthur. Sutherland, who jealously guarded the door of MacArthur's office, icily said no. Brereton, not a forceful man, drove instead to Clark

---

*Colonel Dwight Eisenhower, his former chief of staff, had returned to Washington in 1938 and would soon become a brigadier general on the staff of General Marshall.

Field. There, unknown to MacArthur, sat eighteen of his precious B-17s, lined up on the open field in rows. MacArthur had ordered that all thirty-five of the B-17s in the Philippines be flown to Mindanao, another large island in the Philippines five hundred miles to the south of Luzon. There they would be out of range of Japanese bombers from Formosa.

But, at Brereton's orders, only seventeen of the big bombers had been flown to Mindanao. The remaining eighteen had been kept on Clark Field because space was cramped at the small field on Mindanao.

Near eight o'clock on the morning of December 8, Manila time, some five hours after the attack on Pearl Harbor, American radar screens spotted Japanese planes approaching Luzon. At Clark Field Brereton ordered his eighteen B-17s to take off and orbit the field while his fighters drove off the Japanese attackers. But this first wave of enemy planes swerved away from Clark to strafe and bomb other fields. Brereton, even though his bombers could have stayed aloft for ten hours, ordered them down.

And there they sat in rows as another wave of Japanese planes swooped in on Clark Field They pumped shells into the defenseless Flying Fortresses and picked off American fighter planes as they tried to lift off runways. Within minutes all of the Flying Fortresses and half of the rest of MacArthur's airplanes were smashed and smoking.

What the Japanese had done at Pearl Harbor hours earlier to the Navy's Pacific Fleet—surprised and crippled it—they now had done at Clark Field to MacArthur's air corps. MacArthur no longer had enough bombers to smash the Japanese invasion fleet that steamed toward the Philippines.

America had been shocked by the Pearl Harbor disaster. An investigation began that would end with the courts-martial of the top Army and Navy commanders at Pearl Harbor; both would be fired. But there was never an investigation of the Clark Field disaster. Many historians have said that MacArthur and Brereton also should have been made to stand before the judges of a court-martial.

Asked after the war about Clark Field, MacArthur pointed out that he had ordered all Flying Fortresses flown to safety and thought they had been. He defended Brereton, but said that it was the air commander's job to deploy the bombers—not MacArthur's. ·

That explanation has seemed lame to some critics of MacArthur. They argued that MacArthur was the real commander of the air corps; Brereton was only his deputy who wasn't even allowed to speak to MacArthur in the hours before the attack. In any case, there was no court-martial. One reason probably was the fear in Washington—among Roosevelt and his advisers—that the American people would have been outraged to learn that their generals and admirals had been caught by surprise—not once, but twice—within twenty-four hours.

MacArthur no longer had any bombers to smash the Japanese invasion fleet. The seventeen surviving Flying Fortresses on Mindanao were flown to Australia on the theory that they were now outnumbered and would have been destroyed by superior Japanese air power. MacArthur had to guess where the Japanese would land. He was sure they would pick the shallow Lingayen Gulf, one hundred ten miles from Manila, the place where his father's army had landed some forty years earlier. He was still sticking to the MacArthur plan: to meet the enemy on the beach and hurl him back into the sea.

He had two hundred thousand troops in the Philippines, but only eighty thousand on this main island of Luzon. His critics have argued that he should have pulled all his troops onto Luzon and bunched them in the rugged mountains of the north. There, fighting as guerrillas and living off the land, they might have tied up a Japanese army for years. (Four years later a Japanese army did hole up in those mountains, and it took six months of bloody fighting for MacArthur's men to dig them out.)

But MacArthur wanted to block Japanese ships from Manila's

deep port. He thought—wrongly, as it turned out—that the Japanese could not lunge into southeast Asia without having Manila as a base.

On December 22, as MacArthur had guessed, the Japanese fleet steamed into Lingayen Gulf and in a few days landed some forty thousand troops on Luzon. These tough veterans of battles in China, dashed onto the beaches with a curtain of fire and smoke exploding in front of them.

MacArthur's defenders mainly broke and ran. "They were a mob," said one general of the young Filipinos, many of whom had no helmets and carried guns too old to fire. (MacArthur had pleaded to Washington over the years for new weapons but got only a handful.)

At his headquarters MacArthur grimly read reports of the Japanese army rolling across the flat plains of central Luzon. He sent out a new order: all of his troops on Luzon were to retreat toward the jungles of Bataan. He had switched from the MacArthur plan to the old War Plan Orange.

MacArthur had two armies on Luzon, one in the north under Major General Jonathan Wainwright, a tall, gaunt man whom his men called "Skinny," and another in the south. MacArthur devised a clever "sideslip" maneuver so that both of his armies could pull away from the advancing Japanese and slip into the approaches of the Bataan Peninsula by way of the bridges at Calumpit. If the Japanese could get to the Calumpit bridges before the Americans and the Filipinos, they could cut off the escape into Bataan.

A group of Wainwright's American infantrymen raced to the bridges. They arrived only hours ahead of rumbling Japanese tanks. "Hold Calumpit," MacArthur told Wainwright, "until we have made it across!"

On December 30 the Japanese tanks charged Wainwright's riflemen dug in across the front of the bridges. The infantry knocked out several tanks and the Japanese drew back. But Wainwright knew that more Japanese tanks were massing for another assault. All during the day he anxiously watched as long lines of grimy, bandaged, bedraggled American and Filipino troops tramped wearily across the bridge. Trucks, buses, horse-drawn wagons, even battered taxicabs, carried others over the bridges on the way to Bataan.

On December 31 the Japanese again attacked. And again they were driven back. As dawn broke on New Year's Day, 1942, the last American and Filipino troops crossed the Calumpit bridges. Wainwright gave the signal and his engineers blew them up.

MacArthur's sideslip into Bataan—called "brilliant" by some historians—had succeeded. His eighty thousand troops were lodged in the Bataan jungles. They dug a line across the waist of the peninsula, their artillery and foxholes hidden by the thick foliage. And they outnumbered the Japanese, who had transferred troops from Luzon to storm the British naval bastion at Singapore in southeast Asia.

On December 24 MacArthur evacuated Manila. He, his wife and three-year-old child reached the massive fortress island of Corregidor. He was confident his troops could hold Bataan and Corregidor for six months. That was the length of time he was supposed to resist until the Navy came to lift the siege.

The MacArthurs moved into a small white house on the flat top—called Topside—of the rocky island. His headquarters, filled with radiomen and clerks, was below, in the Malinta Tunnel, one of many that cut through the bowels of "the Rock." There he was visited by General Brereton, who was flying to Australia to build an air force. Saying good-bye, MacArthur grasped Brereton's hand and urged, "I hope you will tell the people outside what we have done here and protect my reputation as a fighter."

"General," Brereton said, "your reputation will never need any protection."

During the next few days Japanese bombers made hourly runs over Corregidor. They dropped tons of bombs onto Topside that shook the tunnels with deafening blasts. Stones and choking dust

77

rained down on soldiers, sailors, marines and Army nurses cowering in the narrow, dark tunnels. And across from the Rock were Japanese troops poised to invade the island.

One day MacArthur asked an aide, Colonel Sid Huff, to find bullets for an old pistol that MacArthur's father had carried in the Philippines. Huff could find only two bullets that would fit the weapon. He gave them to MacArthur. As MacArthur slipped them into the pistol, he said to Huff, "Sid, they will never take me alive."

9

"We Drink of the Same Cup"

The air raid sirens wailed, piercing into the rooms of the MacArthurs' house on Topside. Carrying Arthur in her arms, Mrs. MacArthur rushed outside, followed by her husband. An officer led mother and child to a concrete bunker a few hundred feet from the house.

MacArthur, with his orderly, Sergeant Domingo Adversario, watched his wife and son vanish into the bunker. Then he turned and walked up a small rise to observe the formations of twin-engined bombers approach Corregidor. "Far-off," he later wrote, "they looked like silver pieces thrown against the sun."

MacArthur walked to a nearby anti-aircraft battery and stood next to the gunners as the Japanese planes bombed and strafed Topside. Bombs blew huge, smoking craters in the ground. Smoke and flames and throat-choking dust ringed the two men and the gunners. MacArthur turned and saw the roof fly off his house.

Sergeant Adversario took off his helmet and held it so that half protected the face of the General, who, as usual, wore only his cap on his head. A bomb fragment gashed Adversario's hand. Blood spurted out. But Adversario gripped the helmet as the two leaned against a slight embankment amid the roar of the guns and bombs.

After three hours the bombers swerved away and the din ceased. MacArthur walked to the shelter to see that his wife and child were all right. Then they looked at their blasted, burning house. That night they slept on cots in a rocky nook of the Malinta Tunnel, bare bulbs glaring over their heads.

Each day MacArthur left the tunnel to go outside and stand during bombardments, seeming to defy the Japanese bombs and bullets. "There was nothing of bravado in this," he later declared. "It was simply my duty. The gunners at the batteries . . . they liked to see me with them at such moments."

Yet few men on that beleaguered island would have endured such an ordeal voluntarily. During the bombings of Corregidor in these early months of 1942 soldiers crawled into the tunnels and refused to come out. Even MacArthur had been visibly unnerved. "I feel the General's knees shaking," Sergeant Adversario later told reporter Clark Lee. Yet he continued to walk out into the open whenever enemy bombers droned over Corregidor.

In the early weeks of 1942 MacArthur was confident the Navy would soon send ships to blow away the Japanese. He told his troops: "Help is definitely on the way. We must hold out until it arrives." President Roosevelt himself told the nation and MacArthur's troops via radio that the Navy was busily preparing to come to the rescue. Each day soldiers shinnied up tall trees on Bataan to scan the horizon for the masts of American battleships.

But those battleships were not coming. In Washington there had been agonized conferences among General Marshall, his aide Brigadier General Eisenhower, and naval officers. The Navy, in the person of frosty Admiral Ernest L. King, Chief of Naval Operations, insisted it could not risk the Pacific Fleet's depleted strength to try to lift the Philippines siege against superior Japanese naval might. Reluctantly, Marshall and Eisenhower had come to realize that MacArthur's trapped army was doomed.

On Bataan the Japanese launched attacks that were repulsed by the entrenched Filipinos and Americans. Early in January Mac-Arthur crossed over on a boat from Corregidor to Bataan to visit his front-line soldiers. Carrying a walking stick jauntily, he visited outposts only a few hundred yards from Japanese snipers. With him was General Wainwright, who asked if MacArthur would like to see the heavy guns, hidden behind trees. With a smile, MacArthur replied, by his own account, "I don't want to see them. I want to *hear* them."

He stayed on Bataan only a few hours but what he saw must have depressed him. Looking into his soldiers' emaciated, sunken faces, he knew that they were slowly starving. But he did not seem to recognize their bitterness over the fact that he would not stay on Bataan with them and share this fate.

Though MacArthur's sideslip maneuver had withdrawn his troops safely into Bataan, bungling had left them inadequately supplied. Millions of tons of food that could have fed the Bataan army had been left behind, and most of the Army's trucks and horse-drawn wagons rolled into Bataan empty.

Soon one of every two Bataan soldiers was too sick from near-starvation to fight. "Hunger was with us constantly," one lieutenant wrote. "It wasn't the enemy that licked us. It was disease and the absence of food."

That was MacArthur's first and last visit to Bataan. During the war he named his personal plane the *Bataan* and his staff called themselves "the Bataan Gang," but they and MacArthur had been only a few hours on the peninsula. The Bataan soldiers began to grumble about MacArthur hiding in what they considered the safety of Corregidor. They composed a song to the tune of *The Battle Hymn of the Republic* that included the line: "Dugout Doug lies ashakin' on the Rock, glory, glory. . . ."

MacArthur had openly proved his bravery on the bomb-shattered Rock by leaving dugouts to walk among his gun crews to lift

81

their spirits. Why didn't he visit his Bataan troops more often to lift their spirits? That has puzzled his biographers. One guess might be that, seeing his starved soldiers, MacArthur felt guilt. His switch of plans was one reason why these men were starving. Every general knows that some of his soldiers will die in battle. It is harder for a general to acknowledge that, because of his decisions, some of his soldiers will die of starvation. MacArthur perhaps could not bring himself to go back to Bataan and see those men whose thin faces haunted him for the rest of his life. In his memoirs he wrote of them: "They would grin—that ghastly skeleton-like grin of the dying —as they would roar in unison: 'We are the battling bastards of Bataan—no papa, no mama, no Uncle Sam.'

"They asked no quarter and they gave none. . . . They were filthy, and they were lousy, and they stank. And I loved them."

Shortly after Pearl Harbor and America's declaration of war against Japan and Germany, President Roosevelt promoted MacArthur to the four-star rank of full general—the same rank he had held seven years earlier as Chief of Staff. MacArthur wryly recalled Sergeant Ripley looking for that water hole that was always "about ten miles away" and bellowing, "Thank God, we're holding our own."

By early February MacArthur had come to realize that no help would come. He was bitter toward the Navy. He hinted that the admirals had been so shaken by Pearl Harbor that they were afraid to go to sea. And he talked darkly of Marshall, one of "the Chaumont crowd," favoring General Eisenhower, who would soon be put in command of the Allied Army in Europe. He talked more and more of "the real enemy behind me" in Washington.

In Washington President Roosevelt had met with British Prime Minister Winston S. Churchill. They had decided on an overall strategy for the war. America, England and Russia would first defeat Hitler's Germany. Then they would turn and overwhelm Japan.

General Douglas MacArthur's favorite photograph of himself: smoking a corncob pipe after his return to the Philippines during World War II.

A proud young cadet at the U. S. Military Academy, West Point, 1903.

He loved to strike poses for photographers: Here he is seated, legs dangling, in the chair of the original Lord of St. Benoît Château behind the fighting lines in France during World War I.

He chats with members of his Rainbow Division staff between Beney and
St. Benoît in 1918.

Generals sweat too under stress: As Chief of Staff, MacArthur arrives at a
military checkpoint behind the White House to try to cope with the Bonus
Marchers who have entered Washington. The cool major dragging on a
cigarette at the right is Dwight D. Eisenhower.

Mission accomplished! Under MacArthur's direction U. S. Army troops destroyed these shanties of World War I veterans who came to Washington during the Depression in quest of bonus money for their wartime services. In the background rises the U. S. Capitol.

Opposite: General and Mrs. MacArthur leave Corregidor for the sanctuary of Australia after American resistance to the Japanese invasion of the Philippines crumbles.

These American and Filipino soldiers were not as fortunate as their General after they were overwhelmed on the Bataan Peninsula. Here Japanese troops herd them off to prison camps where many will die.

Having fought his way back to the Philippines from Australia and just landed on Leyte, MacArthur records his famous "I have returned" announcement that was broadcast throughout the world. Note that his uniform is still wet from the landing. At the left, the Filipino leader Sergio Osmena drinks from a canteen.

Once Leyte was secured, MacArthur pushed on to Luzon. Here he and his staff wade ashore at Lingayen Gulf.

MacArthur, at microphone, accepts the surrender of the Japanese aboard the U.S.S. *Missouri* in Tokyo Bay.

After the outbreak of hostilities in Korea, the Commander in Chief flew
there. He inspects troops of the 24th Infantry after landing at Kimpo
Airfield.

MacArthur goes ashore at Inchon with other officers. The Inchon Landing was his last big military coup before President Truman relieved him of command.

The General with his wife and son return home to a warm greeting in America.

That "Europe-first" strategy infuriated MacArthur and his friend, Manuel Quezon, with him on Corregidor. Quezon, racked by the coughs of tuberculosis as he sat in a wheelchair in Malinta Tunnel, told an American officer: "America writhes in anguish at the fate of a distant cousin, Europe, while a daughter, the Philippines, is being raped in a backroom."

In late February General Marshall had a submarine sent to Corregidor to take Quezon, his wife, and a number of other civilians to Australia. Mrs. Quezon urged Jean MacArthur to leave with them.

"No," replied Mrs. MacArthur, "I will stay with the General."

"But what will happen to the boy?"

"We drink," said Jean MacArthur, "of the same cup."

After the Quezons had left, Marshall radioed a message that MacArthur read by the glare of the bare bulbs in the Malinta Tunnel. Marshall suggested that he and his family leave for Australia. MacArthur immediately radioed this reply: "I and my family will share the fate of the garrison."

In the Malinta Tunnel, which was shaken every day by the bombardments, little Arthur—a pale, calm boy—pranced about in a soldier's cap. "The Sergeant" was playing at war. He watched wide-eyed as wounded men were carried into the tunnel on stretchers. His mother chatted with nurses and the few civilian women on Corregidor as if, said one reporter later, "she had endured battle all her life."

The MacArthurs ate the meager half-rations of everyone else on the Rock, mostly canned salmon and rice. MacArthur lost twenty-five pounds and his face was drawn and haggard. One survivor later called Corregidor "a sun-burned, God-cursed land where bombs and shells made life a hell, with death on every hand."

Late in February, a few weeks after MacArthur's sixty-second birthday (his staff and family gave him a small cake), he received a direct order from President Roosevelt. He was told to leave

Corregidor and travel to Australia, there to take command of an Australian and American army being organized to defend Australia.

MacArthur balked at obeying. "I fully expected to be killed," he later told writer Frazier Hunt, who wrote a worshipful biography of him. "I would never have surrendered. If necessary I would have sought the end in some final charge. I would probably have been killed in a bombing raid or by artillery fire. . . . And Jean and the boy might have been destroyed in some final general debacle."

He told Sutherland, his chief of staff, that he would radio Roosevelt and refuse to leave, then join the infantry on Bataan "as a simple volunteer." Sutherland argued MacArthur out of that emotional decision. According to Hunt, Sutherland said, "You are needed in Australia far more than you are needed on Bataan."

After two days of hesitation, MacArthur radioed Washington that he would obey the order. But he requested that he be allowed to pick the date he would leave. Roosevelt agreed.

For almost three more weeks he stayed on Corregidor. To Wainwright on Bataan and to his generals on Mindanao and the other Philippine islands he relayed Roosevelt's orders not to surrender. He told them: "I plan to fight to the complete destruction of our forces on Bataan and then do the same on Corregidor."

MacArthur chose those who would try to escape with him and his family. They included the child's nurse, Ah Chew, the aloof Sutherland and the pompous intelligence officer, Major General Charles Willoughby, who spoke with the accents of his native Germany and was laughingly called by his staff, behind his back, "Sir Charles." Also in the party was Colonel Sid Huff, who had become a personal aide to Mrs. MacArthur.

On the morning of March 10 MacArthur summoned General Wainwright to Corregidor. Sitting together in the musty Malinta Tunnel, MacArthur told Skinny Wainwright that he was leaving. "If I get through to Australia," he told Wainwright, "you know I'll come back as soon as I can with as much as I can. In the meantime you've got to hold."

Wainwright said nothing, well aware that he and his men could not hold out much longer.

The next night, March 11, the party of twenty-two walked through a light rain to the docks on Corregidor. Disliking the confinement of a submarine, MacArthur had chosen to try to escape on the sleek and fast patrol-torpedo boats that were now his only "navy." The seventy-seven-foot long PT boats, powered by huge Packard engines, were designed to flash in on enemy ships, fire torpedos, then flee. Their hulls lightly armored, the PT boats could be blown out of the water by even a destroyer's small guns if they were spotted and caught.

The nineteen men, two women and Arthur clambered onto the four PT boats. On board the lead boat, PT-41, MacArthur took one last look toward the craggy hills of Bataan and the men he was leaving behind.

"I could feel my face go white," MacArthur later recalled. Then he turned to PT-41's skipper, Lieutenant John Bulkeley, and said, "You may cast off, Buck, when you are ready."

Minutes later the four boats, in a diamond formation, nosed out into the waters between Bataan and Corregidor, engines turned low so they wouldn't be heard by Japanese patrol boats. Then, as the dark masses of Corregidor and Bataan fell behind them, the boats roared loudly, engines coughing, and sped out toward a dark and churning China Sea. Some twenty-five hundred miles away was Australia.

10

"I Shall Return"

Little Arthur twisted and moaned at the bottom of the PT boat. He retched, agonizingly seasick. So were most of the other passengers on PT-41, the lone exception being Jean MacArthur.

Ocean spray drenched the passengers as high waves pitched the boat. Its nose flew up to the peaks of waves, slid down the slopes, then was kicked up again by another white-capped wave. As morning light dawned over the tossing Pacific, the General and his family rubbed black and blue bruises. MacArthur later compared the trip to a ride inside a concrete mixer.

Lieutenant Bulkeley steered PT-41 toward the cove of a small island. During the night the four boats had been blown apart by the storm; they had arranged to rendezvous at the island. Already in the cove was PT-32. It carried a party that included MacArthur's lean, mustached signal officer, General Spencer Akin. The skipper of PT-32 saw PT-41 loom out of the morning light and identified it as a Japanese destroyer. "Man the torpedoes," he shouted to his crew.

Sailors aimed the torpedoes at the incoming PT-41. General Akin peered through the morning fog and thought the oncoming craft looked familiar. "Make sure that's a Jap ship before you fire," he called to the skipper.

Moments later PT-32's skipper realized that the approaching boat was PT-41, carrying MacArthur.

Hidden in the cove, the PT boats waited until evening. Then they roared into the gray dusk falling over the Pacific. An hour later Lieutenant Bulkeley, perched high in the cockpit, saw a long gray shape loom out of the darkness and slide across their path.

He cut his engines and ordered silence. MacArthur peered above the cockpit and saw a warship no more than a half-mile away. He thought it was a Japanese battleship. Others identified it as an enemy cruiser.

Ever so slowly, the ship crossed in front of them. Its lookouts almost certainly saw the PT boats bobbing in the water, but probably thought they were native fishing boats. The big Japanese ship melted away into the darkness, and the passengers relaxed.

The sea grew calmer and most of the passengers slept during the rest of the night. About two in the morning MacArthur awoke Colonel Sid Huff and began to talk bitterly about being ordered to leave Corregidor. "But I'll go back there," he told Huff.

"He meant it," Huff later said, "and he was already planning how to do it."

At dawn the boats churned into the harbor of Cagayan, on the north coast of the island of Mindanao. MacArthur scanned the shoreline. He had no way of knowing whether Americans or Japanese troops stood on the beach. Earlier a Japanese patrol had been seen only thirty miles from Cagayan. But American troops still held the town. An American colonel stood on the dock as PT-41 curved toward him. He saw MacArthur's tall figure standing in the bow and was reminded "of Washington crossing the Delaware," he later told D. Clayton James.

The MacArthurs had completed the first five-hundred-sixty-mile

99

leg of their journey. From Mindanao they were supposed to fly to Australia on B-17s. But the Flying Fortresses weren't there, and MacArthur learned that Japanese patrols were picking their way through the jungle only a few miles from Cagayan.

MacArthur, a proud man, obviously felt humiliated by being forced to sneak out of the Philippines like a thief in the night. He might have stayed on Corregidor if his wife and child had not been with him. And he probably fled only after being convinced by the fawning Sutherland that MacArthur, and only MacArthur, could lead back an army to rescue the Philippines. For in MacArthur's mind, as soon would become obvious, there was building an image of himself being fed by his own pride and the worshipful praise of his intimates. That image would soon be displayed by his staff to the world: that MacArthur was the indispensable man in the Pacific. He—and only he—could stop the spread of the Japanese Rising Sun over the Pacific.

In Australia the Army representative pleaded with a Navy admiral for planes to fly the two thousand miles to Mindanao to rescue the MacArthur party. "I'd like to help you," said the admiral, "but it is quite impossible. We need those planes here and can't spare them for a ferry job, no matter how important it is."

On Mindanao an angry MacArthur radioed Washington. General Marshall flashed an order to the admiral in Australia. Three days later two B-17s landed, picked up the MacArthur party, and quickly took off on the long flight over islands held by the Japanese.

Over the island of Timor they were spotted. Japanese fighters rose to intercept them. The Flying Fortress pilots swerved away and lost their pursuers. The Japanese surmised that the bombers were lumbering toward the Australian city of Darwin. The fighters sped for Darwin, dived down and strafed and bombed its airport. But they saw no B-17s. The Flying Fortresses had landed at another airport, at Batchelor field, forty miles away.

Scooting low over the ground, the Japanese fighters roared in on

Batchelor. But they were too late. The MacArthur party transferred to a C-47 transport bound for the inland city of Alice Springs, out of range of the Japanese planes.

"It was close," MacArthur remarked to Sutherland after they had landed, "but that's the way it is in war. You win or lose, live or die—and the difference is just an eyelash."

That kind of statement, reported by MacArthur himself and perhaps true but certainly melodramatic, had become typical of those attributed to him during his years of fame as Chief of Staff and then as the gold-braided field marshal of the Philippine defense forces. At times he seemed almost like an actor on a stage, playing the role of the wise and brave general. In fact, one reporter wrote of him: "If he hadn't been a great general, he would have been a great actor." Sometimes his sycophantic generals sounded like script writers making up lines for a movie star.

Famous though he now was, MacArthur seemed to yearn for even more fame. In his mind he seemed to visualize himself as a giant, and he tried to play that role in actions and words.

The news of his escape electrified Americans already thrilled by his holding of Bataan and Corregidor against the Japanese. Americans had begun to think of Bataan as a victory. "We are holding up the Japanese advance," they told each other, "we are upsetting the Japanese timetable." MacArthur himself told reporters in Australia—and repeated after the war—that Bataan had been a victory because it held up the Japanese drive into southeast Asia.

That wasn't true. The Japanese, after bottling up MacArthur's army on Bataan and Corregidor, had bypassed the Philippines. Their troopships had gone around Manila to carry armies that had captured Singapore and swept through the lands of southeast Asia to the borders of India. Within six months after Pearl Harbor, virtually all of the riches of southeast Asia were theirs, just as they had calculated.

But in America some hailed MacArthur as the Hero of Bataan, even though he had visited his troops there only once for a few hours. They imagined that he had broken out of Corregidor to go to Australia and rally an army that would return to save the Philippines within a few weeks.

MacArthur himself inspired such hopes a few days after his arrival in Australia. Speaking to a group of newspaper reporters, he said solemnly in his dramatic fashion: "I came through and I shall return!"

I shall return!

The words thrilled Americans. They stood and cheered in theaters as they saw newsreels of MacArthur in Australia.

I shall return!

The words rang with strength and the promise of victory. These early months of 1942 had been filled with bad news for Americans: defeats in the Pacific and Asia, defeats in Africa and Russia. But here was one man, MacArthur, who had told the enemy: "I shall return!" And to thrilled Americans those words had a common meaning: that this country and it allies would come back from a string of shattering defeats to win the war.

But there were many other Americans who hated MacArthur for having, as they felt, run out on his doomed men on Corregidor and Bataan. His name was especially anathema among members of the armed forces. In Army training camps it was common to hear the General referred to as "yellow-belly MacArthur" or "Dugout Doug." As had happened in his confrontation with the Bonus Army, his name became a source of great contention among Americans—and it would continue to be so as long as he lived.

MacArthur would soon learn how uphill the road back to the Philippines would be—if he did not know already. Riding on a train to Melbourne, the chief city of this island continent, he asked an American officer how big was the American army in Australia.

102

The officer stared at him blankly. He said, "There are very few troops here." The total was about twenty-five thousand.

MacArthur swung toward Sutherland, "Surely he is wrong," he said. He had expected to find a huge and growing army of Australians and Americans to lead back to the Philippines. In the next few hours he learned that most of America's troops were being trained to go to Europe to fight Hitler. And most of Australia's crack soldiers now battled Hitler's Panzers on the deserts of North Africa. MacArthur didn't have one combat division to block what many expected at any hour: a Japanese invasion of Australia.

When MacArthur learned on that train how little he had to fight with, wrote reporter Clark Lee, he ". . . turned deathly white, his knees buckled, his lips twitched." Later he told Lee: "It was the greatest shock and surprise of the whole damned war."

He was silent for several moments after hearing the news. Then he turned to Sutherland and said, "God have mercy on us."

11

The Road Back: One "Take Buna or Die"

MacArthur sat at the head of a long table. Waiters served small plates of meat and vegetables—these were wartime rations—to men in tuxedos and women in jewels and gowns seated down the sides of the table. At this banquet the Australian government was honoring MacArthur, soon to be formally designated as the Southwest Pacific Area (SWPA) Supreme Commander. Amid the clatter of dishes MacArthur had been telling the people around him of some of the details of his twenty-five-hundred-mile run from Corregidor to Australia. Suddenly one of the guests rose and clinked a spoon against a glass, asking for quiet.

He was Nelson T. Johnson, America's Minister to Australia. "I have just received a message from the President of the United States," he said glancing at MacArthur. "I have been told to announce to General MacArthur that he has been awarded the highest honor his country and mine can bestow—the Congressional Medal of Honor!"

The dinner guests rose and applauded. After twice almost winning it, MacArthur could now wear on his chest that highest of all

American honors. Arthur and Douglas MacArthur had become the first father and son—and the only ones since—to win the Medal of Honor.

In America many still hoped that the Navy would arrive to save the troops on Bataan and Corregidor. They imagined MacArthur storming northward at the head of a mighty army to smash ashore on the Bataan beaches. The nation's two most popular war cries were: "Remember Pearl Harbor!" and "Save the boys on Bataan!"

But early in April, 1942, the pudgy Japanese commander, General Homma, threw waves of fresh troops at the starved Americans and Filipinos on Bataan. There was a week of fighting, and then on April 9, as Wainwright later reported, "a terrible silence" fell over the green jungles of Bataan. And then it was Corregidor's turn to fall to the swarms of Homma's troops. In the tunnels under the Rock were hundreds of wounded soldiers and Army nurses. Knowing his eleven thousand fighting men on Corregidor could not save the wounded and nurses from slaughter, Wainwright radioed President Roosevelt that he would have to surrender "with broken heart . . . but not in shame."

All of the Luzon army of about ninety thousand men had finally put down their rifles. They were lined up by the Japanese and marched off into prisoner-of-war camps. It was the largest American army ever to surrender, this defeat the U.S. Army's worst ever.

In Melbourne MacArthur paced his bare office, furious. When he had been told of Homma's attack, he had ordered Wainwright to counterattack and fight to the mountains of Luzon. After the Bataan and Corregidor collapse, MacArthur hoped that the forty thousand other Filipino and American soldiers still fighting on Mindanao and smaller islands would remain intact to harry the Japanese as guerrillas.

Homma ordered Wainwright to tell all the forces elsewhere in the Philippines to surrender. If Wainwright didn't, Homma hinted, he would slaughter the men and women on Corregidor.

105

"I can't surrender those forces," Wainwright objected. "They are under the command of General MacArthur in Australia."

But Homma showed Wainwright copies of intercepted messages from Washington. They addressed Wainwright as Philippine commander in chief. "You are in command here," Homma told a distraught Wainwright. After some hesitation Wainwright ordered the surrender of all the remaining American and Filipino troops in the islands. Only a handful became guerrillas; the rest surrendered.

In Melbourne MacArthur angrily told aides that this surrender was General Marshall's fault. He had told Marshall, after his arrival in Australia, that he—not Wainwright—should be named commander of the forces in the Philippines. But Marshall had said it would be impossible for MacArthur to command Bataan troops almost three thousand miles away. Now look what had happened. Again "enemies behind me in Washington" had conspired to cripple him.

During the next few weeks MacArthur became even more bitter toward Washington. He had flown to Australia thinking he would command America's Pacific war against Japan. In Washington, however, the Navy had argued that the war against Japan would be fought across nearly six thousand miles of water between Pearl Harbor and Japan. That war at sea, the Navy said, should be commanded by an admiral.

MacArthur fired off cables from Melbourne to argue that there should be a single commander. He was the senior officer in the Pacific, general or admiral. But, he said, he would step aside and be No. 2 under someone else. All he asked, he told Roosevelt and Marshall, is that the Pacific war have a single boss.

But Roosevelt decided to set up two Pacific commands. One would be the Pacific Ocean Area, commanded from Pearl Harbor by the quiet-spoken, calmly efficient Admiral Chester W. Nimitz, chief of the Pacific Fleet. The other theater, the Southwest Pacific Area, would be commanded by MacArthur. Each theater commander would direct his own army, navy and air corps.

MacArthur never ceased being critical of what he called "a divided effort" in the Pacific. (There was only one commander in Europe, he noted grimly: Eisenhower.) After the war he wrote: "Many a man lies in his grave today who could have been saved" had there been one Pacific commander. And, indeed, that divided Pacific command almost did cost him a bloody defeat on the shores of the Philippines some two years later.

As commander of a watery, island-dotted theater some twenty-five times the state of Texas, MacArthur had set himself one overriding goal: to leap from Australia to the Philippines almost three thousand miles away. There, he now knew, a vengeful General Homma had brutally forced MacArthur's men of Bataan and Corregidor on a "death march" across the hot and dusty plains of Luzon. At least five thousand and perhaps as many as eleven thousand Americans and Filipinos died or were killed. Again the faces of the men of Bataan must have come back to haunt Mac-Arthur. One day, he vowed, there would be victories that would allow "the dead of Bataan to sleep well."

But his first task was to defend Australia's seven million men, women and children from a Japanese invasion. The Australian generals had planned to dig a fortified line around the main cities of Australia. MacArthur rejected that concept. He proposed a bolder strategy: a leap north from Australia to the nearby island of New Guinea to check the Japanese advance there and increase his command's holdings. "If successful," in effect he told Washington and his Australian commanders, "this would save Australia from invasion and give me an opportunity to pass from defense to offense . . . move forward, and attack."

By the summer of 1942 MacArthur's army in Australia totaled about two hundred fifty thousand men, mostly Australians, including eight Aussie divisions that had been hastily shipped from Africa.

Ferried from the United States, big Flying Fortresses and fast fighter planes were arriving daily. But most of the five hundred allied planes sat on the runways of Australian airports. Vital parts were missing and mechanics could not find them to ready the planes because of bungling. Bomber pilots paced their barracks while Japanese war ships cruised insolently within sight of Australia's beaches.

That broken-winged air corps was one more weight to depress MacArthur in early summer of 1942. Correspondents saw new lines of worry creep onto his face and often the sixty-two-year-old general's shoulders sagged and he walked dispiritedly. To a friend back home he wrote, "To make something out of nothing seems to be my military fate in the twilight of my service. I have led one lost cause and am trying desperately not to have it two."

Then, from America, arrived a bull-necked bustling fifty-one-year-old general, George C. Kenney. Yelling, cursing, demoting bunglers, Kenney quickly buoyed the spirits of mechanics and pilots. Soon most of MacArthur's bombers and fighter planes droned into the blue skies—"the wild blue yonder" of the Army Air Corps' fight song—to bomb enemy warships.

The arrival of Kenney, wrote war correspondent Clark Lee, had a remarkable effect on lifting MacArthur's spirits. "MacArthur's restoration to full health and activity might well be dated from the day that Kenney walked into his headquarters. . . ."

Two victories at sea, meanwhile, had been the Navy's answer to America's question: "Where is the Navy?" Alerted by codebreakers to the moves of the Japanese Imperial Fleet, the Navy had sunk five enemy aircraft carriers in the Battle of the Coral Sea and the Battle of Midway. The Japanese tidal-wave sweep across the Pacific had been halted—at least for the moment.

MacArthur pleaded with Washington to shift from its defensive stance in the Pacific to the offensive. He suggested an attack on Rabaul, a naval fortress on the island of New Britain, about seven hundred miles north of Australia. If Rabaul were captured, the

Japanese fleet—without a port to refuel—would have to retreat north to the Philippines.

After much acrid debate about who should assault Rabaul—MacArthur's command or Nimitz's—the Joint Chiefs of Staff approved a three-stage plan. Step one would chiefly be directed toward the island of Guadalcanal—by the Navy's marines. Step two would be the capture of islands and areas closer to Rabaul—by MacArthur. Step three would be the assault of Rabaul itself—by MacArthur.

MacArthur was delighted. For the first time, he told his staff, the Pacific war would get the troops, tanks, ships and planes that now streamed across the Atlantic to Eisenhower, who would soon invade North Africa. While the Navy planned to invade Guadalcanal, MacArthur charted his plans to march up the coastline of New Guinea, building bases to attack Rabaul.

New Guinea sits above the northernmost peninsula of the giant island continent of Australia. It is shaped like a squatting dinosaur. Near the tail of the dinosaur on the south coast is Port Moresby, a small and dusty town through which supplies could be funneled to an army advancing northward on New Guinea. From the tail, the "spine" of the dinosaur—the coastline of New Guinea—curves some thousand miles. At the end of that spine is the "head" of the dinosaur, a group of islands only a few hundred miles of water from the Philippines.

To capture additional areas in New Guinea, his springboard toward Rabaul and the Philippines, MacArthur began to land troops in Port Moresby early in July, 1942. He also flew a few engineers across the jungles and mountain peaks of New Guinea to the middle of the "spine"—a small village on the north coast named Buna. To thousands of young Americans and Australians, Buna would soon become a place with another name—death.

MacArthur told his engineers to build an airstrip at Buna so that bombers could take off to hammer at Rabaul. Shortly after the engineers landed at Buna, MacArthur's codebreakers picked up a message to a Japanese admiral. The admiral was ordered to land three thousand troops at Buna. They were ordered to punch their way into the thick jungles of New Guinea, scale a range of mountains that towers above New Guinea—the Owen Stanley Range—and then descend on Port Moresby and MacArthur's thin garrison. They would come through "a back door," so to speak, to capture Port Moresby and sit on Australia's front steps.

The codebreakers notified MacArthur's pompous intelligence chief, Major General Charles ("Sir Charles") Willoughby. He brushed aside the report. He couldn't believe that the Japanese would try to cross impassable jungles and soaring peaks.

Neither could MacArthur. He could have sent troops to Buna to surprise the invading Japanese and blast them into the sea. But he didn't. And to MacArthur's amazement, three thousand Japanese did land at Buna late in July. They swept by the engineers and a few Australian infantry. More than thirteen thousand more Japanese swarmed ashore when Buna was captured. And to MacArthur's and Willoughby's growing astonishment, the Japanese—hauling ammunition and food on their sweating backs—hacked their way through the jungle and began to scale the towering mountains. By mid-September they had scratched over the top of the last peak and almost looked down on Port Moresby. They had done the impossible. For MacArthur, one historian has written, "this was a first-class military disaster."

But even as Port Moresby lay within his grasp, the triumphant Japanese commander had to turn back. His men were exhausted, sick, starving. And on Guadalcanal the Japanese had been furiously trying to dislodge the invading Marines. The Japanese needed more men on Guadalcanal. The Japanese commander above Port Morseby was ordered to go back to Buna so his troops could be shuttled, if needed, to Guadalcanal.

The Japanese crawled and stumbled back to Buna. There,

reinforced by a fleet, they dug fortifications around Buna that were called "a masterpiece" by a U.S. Army historian. "All roads out of the jungle," wrote one American soldier, "ran into streams of fire."

MacArthur—while the Japanese crawled back across the mountains—had rushed two American-Australian divisions into the Buna area by air and sea. They outnumbered the Japanese. But the Japanese stood on high, dry ground while the Allied divisions were mired in the jungle and swamps. The Americans and Australians were hungry, drenched by almost continual rain, sickened by malaria. In the humid heat men sweated off ten pounds in a day. Japanese snipers picked them off where they stood.

In early November MacArthur moved his headquarters from Australia to Port Moresby. He lived in the one-story Government House on a hill overlooking the harbor. Each day he studied reports from Buna, over a hundred miles away. He was becoming angrier and more impatient. Why, he demanded, couldn't those two divisions push the Japanese into the sea?

Australian generals complained that American soldiers wouldn't or couldn't fight in the jungles. That stung MacArthur's pride. And he worried: If the Japanese threw the marines off Guadalcanal, they could send an army across the water to snuff out his divisions trapped in the jungle at Buna.

He also looked over his shoulder at Washington. He knew what Marshall might say: If you can't overwhelm a small Japanese force at Buna, how can you expect to assault Rabaul? What also burned MacArthur was his ambition to beat out the Navy's marines on Guadalcanal and become the first commander to win a land victory over the Japanese.

"Time is of the essence," he angrily told his generals at Buna. He radioed orders demanding progress. His generals radioed back that they needed food, medicine and more guns for their troops.

MacArthur and his staff—not at the scene of so much sickness and despair—didn't believe the generals at Buna. Late in November

MacArthur ordered Lieutenant General Robert Eichelberger to fly from Australia to Port Moresby.

A feisty, studious fifty-six-year-old West Pointer, Bob Eichelberger fascinated war correspondents with combat stories of World War I. After MacArthur, he was the highest-ranking officer in the theater. But MacArthur's staff—and perhaps "Mac" himself, as his staff now called him—had become worried that Eichelberger would get more of the spotlight of publicity than MacArthur. Eichelberger had been banished to train troops in a remote corner of Australia.

But now, on the afternoon of November 30, Eichelberger stepped into MacArthur's hot, sticky office at Port Moresby. He sat down as MacArthur paced the floor and berated his Buna commanders. "A real leader," MacArthur snapped, could win at Buna. He paused and faced Eichelberger. "I am sending you in, Bob. And I want you to remove all officers who won't fight. Relieve regimental and battalion commanders if necessary. Put sergeants in charge of battalions and corporals in charge of companies—anyone who will fight. Time is of the essence; the Japs may land reinforcements any night."

Eichelberger sat silent, unmoving. MacArthur stared at him. "Go out there, Bob," he said slowly, "and take Buna or don't come back alive."

12

The Road Back: Two
Gamble at Los Negros

The mustard-colored DC-3 transport plane revved up its engines, its coughing echoing through the nearby New Guinea jungles. MacArthur and Eichelberger walked toward the plane. MacArthur had calmed down since the evening before. He put a hand on Eichelberger's shoulder and cautioned him to be careful at Buna. "You would be no use to me dead," he said. But as Eichelberger stepped into the plane, MacArthur called out: "Seize Buna no matter what the casualties."

An hour later a taut-faced Eichelberger inspected the American-Australian lines in front of Buna. He saw exhausted, hungry, feverish soldiers who stood knee deep in the water of filthy foxholes. After almost two months in the jungle, the Allied soldiers had been drained of their willingness to fight. When Eichelberger pointed to a Japanese machine gun only a few hundred yards away, a soldier shouted, "Don't shoot at them. They won't shoot at us if we don't shoot at them!"

Eichelberger relieved high-ranking officers and sent them back to Australia. He demanded fresh food and medicine for his troops— and got them from a MacArthur eager to capture Buna. When he had built up his two divisions, Eichelberger launched an all-out assault on Buna. Occasionally he led the way on patrols, gripping a submachine gun. Soon his troops were calling him "Fighting Bob" Eichelberger. "Bloody inch by bloody inch," in Eichelberger's words, the Allied troops wedged their way into Buna. The Japanese stood behind piles of their own dead, wearing gas masks to protect themselves from the stench, as they poured fire at the advancing Americans and Australians.

After two weeks of savage fighting, the Allies penetrated Buna on December 14. But on Christmas Day Eichelberger wrote in his diary that the fighting was "desperate," the outcome still "in doubt." Early in January, 1943, the Japanese retreated from Buna to the beaches. On January 9 an exultant MacArthur flew from Port Moresby back to Australia, where his communiqué writers trumpeted to the world that the Buna campaign was in its "closing phase."

Eichelberger had to swear when he read that. He still faced seven thousand armed and fanatical Japanese for what MacArthur's communiqué writers, in the safety of Australia, called only a "mopping-up operation." Throughout the war MacArthur's claims of "victory" would often be premature and exaggerated.

That "mop-up" of those seven thousand Japanese took more than three weeks. Nearly all were killed—a few drowned, only a handful surrendered. The cost was another thirty-five hundred Allied killed and wounded. When the last shots had been fired, Eichelberger stood at the edge of Buna's military cemetery, lined with white crosses, and wept.

The Buna battle was one of the bloodiest of the Pacific war. MacArthur's communiqués—most written by General Courtney Whitney but inspired by MacArthur himself—talked of "small losses." Actually, one of every eleven Allied soldiers was killed; by comparison, in the savage fighting on Guadalcanal, only one of every thirty-three marines was killed.

MacArthur could now claim the Allies' first land victory over the Japanese (the marine victory at Guadalcanal did not come until February). Millions of Americans read newspaper dispatches from New Guinea of "MacArthur's troops" and assumed he stood at their head in the jungle. He was hailed as "the Miracle General" whom no Japanese could defeat.

Later a bitter Eichelberger wrote to his wife: "The great hero went home [to Australia] without seeing Buna before, during or after the fighting while permitting press articles from his headquarters to say that he was leading his troops in battle."

But Eichelberger also called MacArthur "the most brilliant commander of the Pacific War." In defense of MacArthur's eagerness to put himself in the spotlight and push generals like Eichelberger out of it, his friends argued that this was his way of grabbing America's attention to the war in the Pacific. Because MacArthur was an idol to some Americans, his friends said, President Roosevelt had to send more troops and supplies to the Pacific instead of sending everything to Eisenhower and the Russians. This was an exaggeration. Public opinion had only limited effect on the plans of the Joint Chiefs of Staff.

Back in Australia (he had moved his headquarters from Melbourne to Brisbane, which was nearer New Guinea), MacArthur obviously relished the victory at Buna. At sixty-three, wrote one reporter, "he was the youngest-looking man for his age I have ever seen." His hair was jet black (some said he dyed it). His eyes sparkled and he walked jauntily. His spirits had soared since a year earlier when he had written of being doomed to lead "lost causes."

He and his family lived in a hotel. He was seen only briefly by gawking Australians when he rode in a black Cadillac from the hotel to his headquarters in a nine-story office building seven days a week.

Each morning, as he shaved, he wore a faded brown bathrobe with the West Point "A" he'd won in baseball on its front. His son,

Arthur, would skip into the room. The Sergeant proudly saluted the General and the General snappily returned the salute. MacArthur took his son's hand and they marched around the room "on parade." The General shouted, "Boom! Boom! Boomity-boom-boom!" as he and the boy played soldiers. Then young Arthur put his hands over his eyes until he heard his father shout one loud "Boom!" Arthur opened his eyes and saw his father holding a shiny new toy. The six-year-old Arthur rushed out of the room to yell shrilly at his mother, "Look at the boom-boom papa gave me!"

Each morning his father gave Arthur a new "boom-boom." Sid Huff and Jean had to scour Brisbane's toy stores to keep the boom-booms flowing. Jean once told Huff: "Hide the boom-booms or the General will give them all away at once." On Arthur's birthday, in fact, the boy got one boom-boom for each year of his age.

MacArthur, after breakfast with Arthur and Jean, rode to his office, arriving around ten. He conferred with Sutherland, the only person who could see him without an appointment. Often, alone, MacArthur paced the floor as he pondered a problem. On the floor below, his staff heard his footsteps and told one another, "The Old Man is rug-cutting again."

Around two he left the office. An officer phoned Jean to tell her that he was on his way. He lunched, napped, then returned to the office. It was simply furnished, the walls bare except for a portrait of George Washington. He sat behind a large, cleared desk, facing a chair and a couch. He stayed at the office until late in the evening, often eight or nine o'clock. He insisted that no one—including himself—could leave until every paper on his desk had been taken care of.

Back at the hotel, he and his family, with their sentries, often watched a movie in the living room. MacArthur liked new Western movies and he could sit through two "shoot 'em-ups," as they were called in the 1940s, in one night. "I've never seen him walk out on a

Western," Sid Huff once said, "and there were some pretty bad ones."

In the spring of 1943 MacArthur kissed Jean and Arthur good-bye, one of millions of leave-takings during these years as the war tore families apart. He flew to Port Moresby to live in that ramshackle town as he planned the next stage in the assault on Rabaul.

Each day Kenney's bombers roared off to attack Rabaul and its harbor filled with Japanese ships. One day MacArthur strode into a room in his headquarters where reporters waited. "I have decided," he said in his dramatic way that annoyed many people, "that Rabaul is just about ripe for a knockout blow. I have been hitting the Japanese there for many months now and I think now is the time to give him a haymaker."

The reporters wrote their stories. But later they snickered about how pompously MacArthur used the word "I." "They are always *his* bombers, *his* troops, *his* army," a reporter later said. "You'd think he was fighting the Japanese all by himself."

Back in Washington, during that spring of 1943, Army and Navy strategists studied the shocking casualties of Buna and Guadalcanal. A jungle, they decided, was no place to fight a modern war. By now America's Army and Navy were growing toward ten million men and women. Her factories and shipyards spewed out guns, tanks, planes and ships at a speed the world had never seen nor imagined. In England General Eisenhower organized his armies to invade Nazi-held Europe.

The idea of the Washington strategists concerning the Pacific was simple—"to hit 'em where they ain't," an old baseball tactic. American battleships and carriers could bombard lightly-held enemy islands; then the Japanese garrison would be assaulted by marines and soldiers ferried ashore on flat-bottomed landing craft.

By surprising and capturing such islands, the Allies would cut the lines of supply from Japan to bastions like Rabaul. The bypassed Japanese forces would starve or, as Admiral William F. Halsey would later put it, "wither on the vine." There would be no need for a bloody frontal assault, as at Guadalcanal and Buna, to dislodge fanatical Japanese troops. The Americans would simply go around the bastions, bypassing them, on the road to Tokyo.

In midsummer of 1943 MacArthur was told to cancel his planned "massive, frontal assault on Rabaul." He protested, bitterly disappointed. But soon he began to like the idea of "leapfrogging" over bastions like Rabaul to "island-hop" toward the Philippines.

He was teamed up with Admiral Halsey for these land-sea attacks. The salty Halsey was nicknamed "Bull" by the public after a news story typographical error; everyone in the Navy called him Bill. MacArthur got along with Halsey much better than with most admirals. "Bull Halsey," he once said, "is one of those fighting admirals who doesn't have the old sailor's bugaboo about losing his ships."

Within the next twelve months the team of MacArthur and Halsey surprised and captured a long string of Japanese bases on the curving New Guinea coast and on nearby islands of the southwest Pacific. This was amphibious warfare—troops leaping several hundred miles across water to dash ashore on LCI's and LST's (Landing Craft, Infantry; Landing Ship, Tanks). Some of their boats had wheels that would carry them across land. And above the invaders roared their "umbrella"—the island-based planes of General Kenney, the planes of Admiral Halsey launched from aircraft carriers.

The Japanese were nearly always surprised by these sudden stabs. As a result American casualties were usually, but far from always, light. In one six-month period, MacArthur claimed loss of a thousand six hundred thirty soldiers and marines while killing over twenty-six thousand Japanese. And he had cut off, "to wither on the vine," more than a hundred thousand more, he said.

After the war MacArthur shamelessly claimed credit for the "island-hopping, hit-'em-where-they-ain't" strategy. "In truth," wrote D. Clayton James, in *The Years of MacArthur*, "he strongly opposed that decision [to bypass bastions like Rabaul], but once he was converted, no commander exploited bypassing more brilliantly than MacArthur."

One day early in 1944 General Kenney rushed by General Sutherland and dashed into MacArthur's office. He told the startled MacArthur that one of his pilots had spotted no sign of enemy troops on the small island of Los Negros in the Admiralty Islands. MacArthur rose from his chair, puffing his pipe, and began to pace. He knew well the importance of Los Negros. If he captured it, he would close the ring around Rabaul, some five hundred miles east. That enemy naval base could wither on the vine, as he and Halsey drove northwest toward the Philippines. The Japanese navy then could no longer attack them from the rear.

But MacArthur quickly learned that his intelligence chief, General Willoughby, estimated there were four thousand "armed-to-the-teeth" Japanese in the Admiralties, no matter what Kenney's pilot had said. Whom should MacArthur believe?

Weighing his decision, MacArthur was aware that a bloody defeat or costly victory at Los Negros could hurt him in Washington. The Navy was telling President Roosevelt that its ships should plow straight across the Pacific to invade Japan. MacArthur argued, on the contrary, that he should be allowed to island-hop toward the Philippines, free that country, then spring from there to Japan. The outcome at Los Negros, MacArthur told his staff, could lead Roosevelt to choose the Navy's water-road to Japan as against MacArthur's island-road.

MacArthur ordered the attack on Los Negros, even though he had only about a thousand Americans and Australians for the attack. He had noticed that Japanese commanders, when their island was

119

attacked, did not throw all of their weight at the Allies' first wave when it hit the beaches. They held back most of their force to throw at the Allies if they landed elsewhere, attacks that rarely came. Often, if the Japanese had hurled a full punch at the invaders, they would have pushed the Allies back into the sea. But they didn't and MacArthur gambled that they wouldn't do so at Los Negros.

He decided to go to sea with the invasion fleet. One of his generals, the cautious Walter Krueger, who still spoke with the accents of his native Germany, advised him not to. "It would be a calamity if anything happened to you," Krueger told the theater commander.

"I have to go," MacArthur said.

Before each island invasion, MacArthur had paced in the living room or on the patio of his headquarters, now a lakeside home of a plantation owner in New Guinea. He obviously worried about each landing's success and what it would cost in lives. Now, at least for this one landing, he wouldn't have to pace nervously: he would be there.

He boarded the cruiser *Phoenix*. At sea he was handed a message from scouts who had sneaked onto Los Negros. Their report was succinct: "The island is lousy with Japs."

MacArthur ordered the invasion fleet to sail on. But he told his commanders to flee to the ships if they met heavy fire. And then he would radio Washington that this had been only "a reconnaisance in force" while he hastily beat a retreat.

Dawn spread its red blush over the blue Pacific on the morning of February 29, 1944. As MacArthur watched from the railing of the *Phoenix*, scores of landing craft, churning white wakes, bobbed toward the surf breaking on the white Los Negros beach. MacArthur saw his soldiers splash ashore and heard only the crackle of light fire. As usual, the Japanese had been surprised. And, as MacArthur had hoped, the Japanese commander held back most of his troops, looking for the Allies to swarm ashore somewhere else.

MacArthur turned to an officer in midafternoon and said he would ride ashore. A launch carried him to the beach where he talked with the beachhead commander. "Hold what you have taken," Mac-Arthur told him, "no matter against what odds. You have your teeth in him now. Don't let up."

From the jungle facing the beach came the chatter of machine guns and the dull roar of exploding mortar shells. Officers in steel helmets ran alongside MacArthur as he calmly strolled the beach. He was dressed in suntan pants and open-necked shirt, four stars on his collar, the gold "scrambled-eggs" embroidery on the bill of his floppy cap. Officers excitedly told him there were Japanese snipers hidden in the treetops only a hundred yards away. They could line up the famous general in their gunsights.

MacArthur said nothing as he examined shell holes. One officer tapped him on the elbow and pointed toward the jungle. "Excuse me, sir," he said, "but we killed a Jap sniper in there just a few minutes ago."

"Fine," MacArthur said, going toward the jungle. "That's the best thing to do with them."

He stopped at the corpses of two Japanese snipers, slain only minutes earlier. "That's the way I like to see them," he said to a helmeted soldier who was warily pointing his M-1 rifle at the treetops.

MacArthur stayed on the beach for two hours in a pelting rain. Then, "wet, cold, and dirty with mud up to the ears," he returned to the *Phoenix*. Before leaving the beach he told his commanders to expect an all-out "banzai" attack that night, now that the Japanese knew there would be no landings elsewhere. That night the Japanese did attack and were repulsed, the beachhead now fortified with American troops. Within a month all the Admiralties had been taken and MacArthur could later state:

"Rabaul was now securely encircled—the noose was complete.

More than eighty-thousand Japanese troops were now choked off. . . ."

Congratulations poured into MacArthur's jungle headquarters in New Guinea from all over the world. From Washington, Admiral King, who disliked MacArthur intensely, called the attack "brilliant." From London, Britain's Prime Minister Winston Churchill radioed his "every good wish, my dear MacArthur."

MacArthur's careful general, Walter Krueger, called Los Negros "a brilliant strategic move and fortunately successful. But if it had not been and General MacArthur had been killed or captured, by no means a far-fetched idea, it would have been a disaster. . . ."

Island-hopping and bypassing in other areas were eventually to carry MacArthur to Hollandia on the north central coast of New Guinea and ultimately to Morotai Island, northwest of New Guinea. On Morotai, about fifteen hundred miles from Port Moresby, MacArthur's troops stood only a few hundred miles away from the Philippines and the men of Bataan, half starved behind barbed wire.

Yet MacArthur grumbled constantly that he wasn't getting his fair share of troops and supplies while Eisenhower, poised to invade France, was getting everything. "I have done the best with what I have," he wrote in self-pity to a friend, "but no commander in American history has so failed of support as here. We have come through, but it has been shoestring stuff."

In truth, he had indeed got only shoestrings at the beginning of the war. But by midsummer of 1944 there were about a million eight hundred thousand GIs in Europe and about the same number in the Pacific (but only about one-third of them in MacArthur's theater, the other two-thirds being under Admiral Nimitz). While some eight thousand eight hundred American Air Force planes set Germany aflame, about seven thousand nine hundred bombed the Japanese in the Pacific. And the bulk of the American Navy was in the Pacific. The balance of American power, by 1944, was almost evenly divided between the Pacific and Europe.

Nevertheless, MacArthur's deep distrust of Marshall and the Navy grew blacker. "There are some people in Washington," he said glumly, "who would rather see MacArthur lose a battle than America win a war." In the summer of 1944 his mood became even darker when he learned that Marshall and Roosevelt seemed to favor the Navy's plan to thrust across the Central Pacific into the heart of Japan. The Philippines would be bypassed.

In angry cables to Marshall, MacArthur protested: How could we forget seventeen million Filipinos and the caged Bataan survivors? Marshall gently reminded him that they would be freed as soon as Japan surrendered.

MacArthur was not appeased. He had fought within almost touching distance of the Phillipines, that nation and people so dear to them, those men of Bataan he'd left, all those people to whom he had solemnly promised: "I shall return!"

Now his promise to return was being torn into scraps by Washington. MacArthur was infuriated. He begged Marshall to be allowed to fly to Washington to present his case personally to the President. On July 26, 1944, he got a cable from Marshall. He was told to fly to Pearl Harbor to meet "a Mr. Big."

MacArthur knew who Mr. Big would be—the President. As he boarded his personal B-17, *Bataan* inscribed on its nose, MacArthur suspected that President Roosevelt was headed for Pearl Harbor to try to decide between the Navy's strategy and MacArthur's. This would be MacArthur's last chance to make good his promise that had echoed and reechoed around the world: *"I shall return!"*

13

The Road Back: Three
"I Have Returned!"

The heavy cruiser *Baltimore* lumbered by the antisubmarine nets and nosed into Pearl Harbor, her long slate-gray guns glinting in the morning sun. Sailors tied the big ship to a dock as Pacific Fleet Chief Admiral Chester N. Nimitz and his seagoing commander, Bill Halsey, strode up the gangplank. On the deck of the *Baltimore* they saluted their commander in chief, President Roosevelt.

Roosevelt sat in a wheelchair, a cigarette holder poking out of his mouth. Grinning, he asked the admirals, "Where's Douglas?"

Nimitz and Halsey said they didn't know, but that MacArthur's plane, the *Bataan*, had landed a few hours earlier. As the men chatted, they heard the wail of sirens from the dock. Officers rushed to the railing of the *Baltimore*. They saw a long, open limousine screech to a stop. In the back of the limousine, alone and in grandeur, sat MacArthur in his floppy hat and a leather flying jacket.

Soldiers and sailors on the dock applauded. With long strides MacArthur went up the gangplank to the deck and saluted the President.

"Hello, Doug," the President said, enough of an actor himself to know he had lost the spotlight. Teasingly, he glanced at the leather

124

jacket and said, "What are you doing with that leather jacket on—it's darn hot today."

"Well, I've just landed from Australia," MacArthur said nonchalantly to the President. "It's pretty cold up there."

That dramatic entrance by MacArthur may have been his way of meeting the President on even terms. Many Republican leaders hoped to nominate MacArthur to run against Roosevelt in the elections in the fall of 1944, only a few months off. They had written to MacArthur and MacArthur had smiled at the idea. "My Chief talked of the Republican nomination . . ." General Eichelberger recorded in his diary. "I can see that he expects to get it. . . ." MacArthur's aide, Sid Huff, once said, "the idea [of running] wasn't unpleasant for MacArthur."

In letters to Republicans early in 1944, MacArthur had talked critically of Roosevelt and his New Deal ideas. Angry Democrats had demanded that Roosevelt fire MacArthur for being "disloyal" to his commander in chief. But Roosevelt said nothing. And the MacArthur-for-President boom began to wither. In a Wisconsin primary election for delegates, MacArthur had got very few votes. On New Guinea after that election an embarrassed MacArthur began to back away from any idea that he wanted to be President. "I am not a candidate for the office nor do I seek it," he told reporters, but most of them believed he had hoped for it before the Wisconsin setback.

Now, at Pearl Harbor, MacArthur—with that dramatic entrance—seemed to be saying to the President: "I am no ordinary theater commander like Nimitz and don't treat me as one. I am not a Presidential candidate, but I am the Army's senior general."

The evening of his arrival in Pearl Harbor, Roosevelt called Nimitz and MacArthur together for a conference. The brisk Nimitz spoke first, outlining the Navy's argument for a jab across the Central Pacific and a landing on the island of Formosa (today called Taiwan) that Japan had wrested from China in 1895. Formosa

125

would be a base for the leap into Japan. When Nimitz finished speaking, Roosevelt glanced toward MacArthur at the other end of the table. "Where," he asked, "do we go from here?"

The Philippines, MacArthur replied emphatically. He gave his reasons why. There were three hundred thousand Japanese soldiers on the Philippine islands of Mindanao and Luzon. They could spring north to attack Americans landing in Formosa, MacArthur said. And just as important, America had a "moral obligation" to free the Filipino and American POWs.

Alone later with the President, MacArthur was even more emphatic. Staring at Roosevelt across a dining room table, he snapped: "You cannot abandon seventeen million loyal Filipino Christians to the Japanese in favor of first liberating Formosa. . . . American public opinion will condemn you, Mr. President. And it would be justified."

The President did not reply. MacArthur glanced at him. He had been startled by the President's appearance. He was gaunt, his face ashen. "Physically," MacArthur later wrote, "he was just a shell of the man I had known. It was clearly evident that his days were numbered."

The next day Roosevelt asked MacArthur to ride alone with him in his open car as they reviewed troops. Roosevelt asked MacArthur what he thought the President's chances were of winning a fourth term in the fall elections.

MacArthur replied that he was no politician. Roosevelt might have smiled at that but he said nothing. MacArthur added that Roosevelt was a big favorite with the troops. "This," MacArthur said later, "seemed to please him greatly."

The next day they said good-bye, these two giants of their time—alike in many ways in their dominant personalities, unalike in their views. They would never meet again.

When Roosevelt returned to Washington, he and his Joint Chiefs of Staff seemed unable to decide between MacArthur's and the Navy's Pacific strategy. During that summer and fall of 1944 all eyes of the nation were fixed on Europe, where General Eisenhower's armies streaked across France toward Germany, spearheaded by General George Patton's tanks. Many Americans thought they would celebrate victory over Hitler by Christmas of 1944. Then the might of Russia, Britain and America could fall like a hammer on Japan.

MacArthur and his staff, meanwhile, drew up a timetable to invade the Philippines. First he would invade the smaller island of Leyte around Christmas, then Mindanao and finally attack Luzon and the Philippine capital, Manila. Halsey had been steering his battlewagons and aircraft carriers into Philippine waters to blast away at the Japanese fleet. One of his pilots was knocked down over Leyte. Natives rescued him and told him there were only a few Japanese troops on the island.

Halsey flashed the news to Nimitz in Pearl Harbor and urged an immediate attack on Leyte. Nimitz sent the idea to the Joint Chiefs in Washington and they approved.

MacArthur was delighted. His timetable for the invasion of Leyte had been moved up almost three months. And by its approval of the attack on Leyte, Washington had signaled that the attack on Japan would be launched from the Philippines—not Formosa.

On October 14, 15 and 16 one of the largest armadas ever to float on the Pacific Ocean—almost a thousand ships loaded with a hundred seventy-four thousand troops—covered the horizon as it plowed from New Guinea toward Leyte. Aboard the cruiser *Nashville* was MacArthur, his cabin decorated with framed photos he always carried with him—of his father, mother, brother, wife and son.

On the night of October 18 the *Nashville* steamed into Leyte Gulf. MacArthur paced his cabin until early in the morning. He awoke at dawn to hear the roar of the *Nashville's* guns. Dressed in his suntan trousers and open shirt, the four gold stars gleaming on the collar ends, he stood on the *Nashville's* bridge and peered into a gray mist toward the shores of the Philippines. He could see the docks of Tacloban, where he had stepped ashore fresh out of West Point some forty years earlier.

The Navy's big guns poured shells and fiery rockets onto the beaches of Leyte. Smoke and flame leaped from the green jungles. Suddenly, on the bridge, MacArthur saw a black periscope poke out of the water. The *Nashville* swung left and then right to dodge torpedoes as Navy destroyers swerved by to drop depth bombs. The periscope disappeared.

Above Leyte thundered almost a thousand planes from Navy carriers. Like angry bees they buzzed the beaches. General Kenney's planes were not roaring above MacArthur's troops for this invasion; they could not fly this far from their airstrips on New Guinea. MacArthur depended on the Navy for his air cover.

Landing craft, jammed with soldiers and marines, churned toward the beaches on October 20. There they were pinned down by diving Japanese Zekes. Navy Corsairs and Cougars roared in and soon there were hundreds of dogfights in the blue sky over a smoking Leyte. Japanese bombers lifted off from nearby Luzon fields to hurtle down bombs on the American ships jammed into Leyte Gulf. From *Nashville's* bridge MacArthur watched the bombers come out of the smoke-obscured sun, dip and turn to evade the sheets of flame being thrown up at them by the fleet's antiaircraft gunners. Huge geysers of water spouted high as exploding bombs blasted the waters around the *Nashville*. MacArthur could see smoke rising from damaged and sinking ships.

The surprised Japanese had hastily reinforced Leyte. They knew that if the island fell, a very large part of their troops in the southern Philippines would be cut off. They also knew that MacArthur had come to Leyte with no land-based planes. Wisely, they chose to fight

128

for the Philippines on Leyte. If it fell, they could still fight a last-ditch battle on Luzon, but then their backs would be to the sea, no place to go, cut off from Japan by the American Navy. "I knew," MacArthur wrote later, "it [Leyte] was to be the crucial battle of the war in the Pacific." It would be crucial because if the Japanese lost Leyte, they had, in effect, lost the Philippines. And without the Philippines they would be cut off from southeast Asia and the oil they needed to go on fighting. Lose Leyte, the Japanese knew, and they had lost the war.

And so the Japanese were funneling everything—planes, their troops and soon their Imperial Navy—into Leyte.

Amid the deafening blasts of guns and the shrieks of diving planes, MacArthur watched his troops fight their way inland at two main points, "Red" and "White" beach. Near noon he turned and announced he would ride into Red Beach with the third wave of troops.

He boarded a launch with the Philippines' President-in-exile, Sergio Osmeña (several months earlier Manuel Quezon had died in the United States of tuberculosis). Next to MacArthur was Dick Sutherland, who had escaped with him from these Philippines almost three years ago. As the launch chugged toward the smoke and clatter of the battle on the beach and nearby jungle, MacArthur said grimly to Sutherland, "Well, believe it or not, we're here."

The launch bumped onto a sand pit some fifty yards from shore and was stuck. MacArthur stepped out of the boat into knee-deep water and sloshed toward shore. He saw infantrymen hugging the beach as Japanese bullets whizzed out of the jungles.

Face grim, he walked onto the beach, seawater squirting out of his shoes. A combat photographer snapped his picture. That picture of a grim MacArthur marching out of water onto the Philippines would be spread the next day onto newspapers all across America. And over it was the huge headline:

MACARTHUR RETURNS!

129

On the beach riflemen stared in amazement as the man some still reviled as "Dugout Doug" strode erectly toward them, smoking his pipe. One GI was infantryman Jan Valtin, who was crouched behind a tree. Later he wrote: "He walks along as if the nearest Jap snipers were on Saturn instead of in the palm tops a few hundred yards away. You stare, and you realize that you are staring at General Douglas MacArthur."

One soldier shouted at another: "Hey, there's General MacArthur!"

The other, his face burrowed in the sand, muttered, "Sure, and I suppose he's got Mrs. Roosevelt with him."

But it was MacArthur who walked to a radio transmitter set up on the beach. Rain pattered on his shoulders and cap as he spoke into the microphone:

"People of the Philippines! I have returned!"

I have returned! The words were flashed to America. That promise, made in the depths of defeat almost three years earlier, had been kept. All across the Philippines and America, people thrilled at the news of the kept promise: *I have returned!* Douglas MacArthur was called America's Man of the Hour.

MacArthur stood erect as the American and Philippine flags were hoisted over Philippine soil for the first time since they had been jerked down over Corregidor almost three years ago. In many ways this may have been his most glorious hour.

But beyond the horizon steamed a huge fleet of Japanese battleships and cruisers. They lumbered toward Leyte Gulf, where they would soon give MacArthur his most suspenseful hours of the war.

14

The Bullet That Has Not Been Cast

"All my life I have been reading and studying naval combat," MacArthur said with obvious eagerness. He looked across his desk at the admiral, who had just told him of the impending sea battle. "The glamor of sea battle," MacArthur went on in his pontificating tone, "has always excited my imagination."

He was speaking to Admiral Thomas Kinkaid, his broad-shouldered naval commander. The two were seated in MacArthur's office in a white house in Tacloban, not far from Red Beach, where MacArthur had landed on Leyte a few days earlier. Above them a wooden ceiling fan turned slowly in the humid heat. Kinkaid had just told MacArthur the details of a report from the codebreakers, who had picked up a message that the main elements of the Japanese Imperial Fleet were steaming for Leyte Gulf and a showdown battle. It was a big gamble for the Japanese to send their battle wagons against the powerful Third Fleet of Halsey and the Seventh Fleet of Kinkaid which had been assigned to screen the Leyte landings.

But the Japanese strategists felt this risk had to be taken. If Leyte was lost, the Philippines were doomed. With this last desperate punch, the Japanese hoped to eradicate MacArthur's army jammed onto the cramped Leyte beachhead.

A silvery-haired man who didn't often argue with his boss, Admiral Kinkaid had suddenly turned stubborn. No, he said, MacArthur could not go on the *Nashville* to watch the sea battle with the Imperial Fleet. Kinkaid would not take the responsibility of risking his theater commander's life. If MacArthur insisted on boarding the *Nashville*, Kinkaid said, eyes flashing, he would keep the cruiser out of the line of battle.

Grumbling, MacArthur agreed to stay ashore. "For some reason," he later said of Kinkaid and of his own staff, "they felt that a sixteen-inch naval shell represented a greater peril to my person than all the tons of steel that the enemy was directing at the beachhead."

On October 23, as the Japanese fleet moved closer, the naval commanders shaped their plans for the battle and kept MacArthur informed. Halsey's Task Force 34 would guard the narrow San Bernardino Strait, a channel that was the "doorway" to Leyte Gulf. With Task Force 34 as sentry, the Japanese fleet could not crash down on MacArthur's army on the beach at Leyte.

But the Japanese admirals had devised a shrewd plan. Their fleet would split into three task forces. A Northern Force would commit suicide by being "bait." It hoped to attract Halsey's Task Force 34 and then run. If Halsey chased the bait, he would leave Kinkaid's smaller Seventh Fleet alone to guard Leyte. Then the Imperial Fleet's two other task forces, the Central and the Southern, could crash through Kinkaid and blast away at MacArthur's ships and troops as they sat helplessly in Leyte Gulf and on the beaches.

On the morning of the 23rd one of the three Japanese task forces, the Southern, was located by the codebreakers. Admiral Kinkaid's Seventh Fleet ambushed it on October 24 in the Battle of the Sulu Sea and virtually wiped it out. Only one destroyer limped away.

Halsey heard by radio of Kinkaid's victory. His pilots had spotted the Northern Force—the "bait." Halsey swung his ships north to

132

give chase. He was sure that Kinkaid now could guard Leyte alone. By the evening of the 24th not even an American rowboat patrolled the San Bernardino Strait. The powerful Japanese Central Force, commanded by Admiral Takeo Kurita, snaked into the narrow channel, its radios silent.

That night Admiral Kinkaid, aboard his flagship, wanted to reassure himself that Halsey was where he was supposed to be. At dawn on the 25th he radioed Halsey: "Is Task Force 34 guarding San Bernardino Strait?"

The delayed reply came three hours later. Kinkaid and MacArthur read it with grim faces: "Your 241912 negative. Task Force 34 is . . . now engaging enemy carrier force."

By now a horrified MacArthur and Kinkaid knew the strength of Kurita's Central Force—four battleships, six cruisers, and eleven destroyers, some of the battlewagons packing the world's heaviest guns. Facing it was a Seventh Fleet made up mostly of light aircraft carriers and destroyers.

At his house in Tacloban MacArthur could only pace and wait. His troops were being bombed and strafed by Japanese planes. Without air cover they could not move and were mired amid driving rains in Leyte's mud. And the Seventh Fleet's airplanes were now pointed toward Kurita's onrushing armada. MacArthur had liked the idea of the long leap from Morotai to Leyte—a three-day sea voyage—but now he longed for General Kenney's land-based fighters.

At seven o'clock on the morning of the 25th, amid sudden rain squalls, Kinkaid's destroyers raced bravely toward the huge Japanese battleships and cruisers. The destroyers tried to hide behind smokescreens as they peppered the enemy with their shells. Within minutes an American destroyer and light carrier had been hit and set aflame. Other carriers had their decks ripped open by enemy shells and diving fighters.

American fighter pilots took off to torpedo and skip-bomb the Japanese ships. They dove into curtains of deadly fire. Surviving

133

pilots could not land on the ripped and burning decks of their carrier. They had to crash-land into Tacloban's mud while MacArthur watched "the endless stream," as he later said, "with aching heart."

Kinkaid radioed to Halsey for help. There was no reply. Halsey was intent on his target, the "bait" carriers of the Northern Force. In Hawaii Admiral Nimitz heard Kinkaid's frantic calls. Nimitz radioed Halsey: "The whole world wants to know where is Task Force 34?"

Halsey replied he was sinking carriers. Nimitz ordered him to turn south to Leyte. Reluctantly Halsey turned south. He left blazing the remnants of the Northern Force; its brave but suicidal job had been well done.

On Leyte MacArthur heard the approaching roar of Kurita's guns. He knew that Halsey wouldn't arrive for almost twelve hours. By then Kinkaid's tiny force would be sunk and Kurita's ships could roam Leyte Gulf, sinking MacArthur's troopships. Their shells would turn the Leyte beachhead into a smoking red hell. American and Australian troops were trapped—the Japanese army planted in front of them, the big guns of the Japanese navy at their backs.

Then suddenly—to the amazement of Kinkaid and MacArthur—the Japanese ships spun around and fled toward the San Bernardino Strait. Admiral Kurita had picked up Halsey's message that he was coming back with his carriers. Kurita feared that his ships would be bottled up and sunk in Leyte Gulf.

They might have been. But if Kurita had stayed to smash MacArthur's troops and ships, he would have crippled the American offensive in the southwest Pacific. The Philippines would have stayed in Japan's hands for at least another six months before MacArthur could put together another invasion force. "If there had been a Bull Halsey in command of the Japanese fleet instead of a Kurita," one historian later wrote, "the battle of Leyte Gulf would have been a smashing Japanese victory."

It had been a close call for MacArthur. The situation had been

134

saved, an American admiral said shortly afterwards, due in part to "the definite partiality of Almighty God."

Some of MacArthur's officers blamed Halsey for chasing the bait. At dinner one day MacArthur overheard an officer assail Halsey.

MacArthur pounded a fist on the table. "That's enough!" he shouted. "Leave the Bull alone. He's still a fighting admiral in my book."

To MacArthur the blame for the near catastrophe could be put "squarely at the door of Washington." "Two key commanders [Halsey and Kinkaid]," he later wrote, "were independent of each other, one under me and the other under Admiral Nimitz 5,000 miles away." Leyte Gulf, he wrote, proved "the dangers involved in the lack of a unified command."

With his rear now safe, MacArthur began to direct his troops— commanded by General Krueger—as they pushed across Leyte. His headquarters was the white two-story house in Tacloban. A concrete air-raid bunker had been built on the front lawn. MacArthur ordered the bunker carted away. "It spoils the looks of the lawn," he told Kenney.

"I didn't think it made much sense . . .," Kenney said. "I had tried to get him into dugouts before without much success."

Japanese planes zoomed low over Tacloban night and day to bomb and strafe. An easy target, the white house soon was pockmarked by shell fragments. One day an American antiaircraft crew, blasting away at a bomber, fired too low. Their shell crashed into MacArthur's empty bedroom. The shell was a dud and didn't explode. The next morning MacArthur placed the defused shell on the table of the gun crew's commander and said, smiling, "Bill, ask your gunners to raise their sights just a little bit higher."

One evening a Japanese Zeke swooped low over Tacloban and poured tracer bullets through MacArthur's office, which happened to be empty. When MacArthur returned in his Jeep from the front, an aide showed him where the bullets had chipped the wall. He turned away, saying, "The bullet that has been designed for me has not been cast."

One day he stood in the office with some aides during an air raid. He was jabbing at wall maps with a pointer when a bomb exploded near the house. Walls and floors trembled and clouds of dust poured through the open windows.

MacArthur finished the sentence he had started, his hand still steady on the pointer. Then he told his aides, "Better look in the kitchen and outside. That bomb was close, and someone may have been hurt."

The bomb had been close. It had wrecked the kitchen and injured at least three people.

"MacArthur's behavior did not surprise those who had seen him on Corregidor," D. Clayton James has written, "but his calmness and courage astonished other [headquarters] personnel who had not been with him under fire."

One who was astonished was his personal cook—"my red-headed cook," MacArthur affectionately called him. He was Sergeant Fred DaTorre. During another air raid, all the cooks fled the house. DaTorre stayed. As explosions shook the paintings on the walls, DeTorre heard the tinkle of piano music coming from the dining room. He peeked in. He saw MacArthur tapping the keys of the piano. Their eyes met but DaTorre realized that MacArthur was lost in the classical music he was listening to in his mind.

"He was the finest man I ever met," DaTorre said thirty-five years later when he was a waiter in a New York restaurant. "He was very concerned about his men. He paced for hours before an invasion, worrying. He went out onto battlefields to see with his own eyes what was going on. And back at headquarters he never had any big parties, as some of the officers did."

DaTorre, like most men who served close to MacArthur, felt a mixture of love, respect and awe for "Mac" and "the Old Man," as they called him. "He always requested, he never ordered," Da-

Torre remembered. "And he always showed his gratitude. Once we had to travel overnight to another camp. We arrived late in the afternoon. There was no time to set up a field kitchen. But I was able to serve a nice hot dinner of soup and fried chicken I'd brought along. He took the time to thank me and called me a genius in the kitchen. How many men of his high position would have taken the time to say thanks?"

MacArthur once told DaTorre that a bowl of soup was too salty. Nettled, the cook replied that the General must have put in too much salt without tasting it.

Immediately the General was apologetic. "You're right, Sergeant," he said. "Now I remember. I did put in salt."

"He liked simple cooking," DaTorre remembered. "Always the same breakfast—three eggs sunny side up, three strips of bacon, orange juice, toast, jelly and coffee. For lunch he especially liked my grilled American cheese sandwiches. At dinner he liked poultry like squab with a dish of guava jelly.

"He really loved orange juice. He drank a quart a day. Sometimes, at night, I'd hear a noise in the kitchen. It was the General. He'd be up raiding the icebox for a glass of orange juice."

By now, midautumn of 1944, MacArthur had not seen his wife and son, back in Australia, for more than a year. He could have flown to Australia for a short visit. But he didn't. He shared the experiences of millions of Americans during those war years—separation from loved ones. Almost every day he wrote to Jean and the boy, as far as is known always signing the letters "MacArthur." Even to a wife and son he was never Doug or Douglas or Daddy.

Just before Christmas, 1944, as MacArthur's troops were locked with the growing Japanese army on Leyte amid howling typhoons, news came from Washington that President Roosevelt had signed legislation promoting him to the new five-star rank of General of the Army. Six others also were given five stars, the most ever worn by an American officer. They were General Marshall, General

137

Eisenhower, General "Hap" Arnold of the Air Force, Admiral King, Admiral Nimitz, and Admiral Leahy (the naval appointees were termed Fleet Admiral). MacArthur proudly pointed out to intimates that he outranked them all, having held the rank of four stars longest. He was especially delighted that he was designated as senior to Eisenhower, whom he privately disparaged as "the best clerk I ever had." With war correspondents he was openly critical of Eisenhower's defeat in Belgium late in 1944 at the Battle of the Bulge.

Often MacArthur—with an eye on having his name and pictures in magazines and newspapers back home—talked to correspondents. Turner Catledge of *The New York Times* later wrote of him: "As he spoke, he was variously the military expert, the political figure, the man of destiny . . . we had never met a more egotistical man, no one more aware of his egotism, and more able and determined to back it up with his deeds."

In early December of 1944 the Leyte commander, General Krueger, came up with an idea: a landing by sea at the port of Ormoc, about thirty miles west of Tacloban on the opposite coast of Leyte. If Ormoc were captured, he pointed out to MacArthur, he would be in a position to cut the Japanese army on Leyte in two. And the Japanese would no longer be able to pour in fresh troops.

MacArthur thought about the move. He pondered problems of strategy much like a chess player. "Now if we do this," he would say to his staff, "they might do this or if they were clever they might do that. Now if they do so and so, we should answer one of three ways." He would tick off the three ways. Then he would list the six, seven or eight things the Japanese might do to retaliate. Out of that spider-web kind of thinking would come his decisions.

He approved Krueger's idea to land at Ormoc (in his memoirs he claimed it as his own). On December 7, 1944, three years after Pearl Harbor, the American 77th Division rode ashore at Ormoc and routed the surprised Japanese. That amphibious landing doomed the seventy-six-thousand-man Japanese army on Leyte. But they fought on for more than four months, holed up in mountain caves. Only about eight hundred surrendered. The rest were killed, drowned or died of starvation.

For the Americans and Australians on Leyte, the cost had been over fifteen thousand casualties, including more than three thousand dead. Several years later the Japanese Emperor Hirohito told MacArthur that the defeat on Leyte convinced him that the war was lost.

A year earlier MacArthur had been fifteen hundred miles away on New Guinea. Now he stood in the heart of the Philippines. Less than a hundred miles distant from the northern end of Leyte loomed southern Luzon. On Luzon were the imprisoned men of Bataan and Corregidor. MacArthur began to plan for the battle of Luzon, his last of World War II.

15

"Let No Enemy Ever Haul Them Down"

"Man battle stations . . . man battle stations. . . ."

The order klaxoned out of the cruiser's loudspeakers. Sailors clattered up steel ladders to rush across decks to their gun positions. MacArthur stood near twin-barreled antiaircraft guns on the quarterdeck of the cruiser, the *Boise*. He puffed calmly on his long-stemmed corncob pipe. The *Boise* swerved and MacArthur watched the long white wake of a torpedo churn toward the ship and narrowly miss it.

The *Boise* was one of nearly a thousand American ships sailing west toward Luzon and its capital of Manila on this day early in January of 1945. The armada carried nearly two hundred thousand Americans and Australians, the largest army yet assembled in the Pacific. On Luzon's beaches waited about the same number of Japanese.

The Japanese had seen the armada coming. Out of Manila slipped subs to loose torpedoes at the zigzagging American battleships, carriers and cruisers. And from the sky roared a terrifying new weapon—the Kamikazes or "suicide pilots." They crouched in their cockpits as they dived through antiaircraft fire in the often successful attempt to smash into the decks of warships, blowing up themselves and their targets. A week earlier, during an Allied invasion of

Mindanao, a Kamikaze had plowed into the *Nashville*, killing a hundred thirty-three and injuring a hundred ninety. MacArthur had wanted to watch that invasion from the *Nashville*; he had been persuaded not to go only at the last minute.

Now this Luzon-bound armada was being buzzed by hundreds of Kamikazes and harried by pursuing subs. The trips from Leyte and New Guinea, one historian later wrote, were "a nightmare."

At dawn on January 9 the armada slid into Lingayen Gulf, where the Japanese had landed three years earlier. Like blackbirds the Kamikazes rose from Luzon to smash at the ships squeezed together in the gulf. On the *Boise*'s bridge MacArthur was told that the Kamikazes had hit a battleship and two cruisers.

Amid the thunder and flame of the fleet's guns, landing craft streaked toward shore carrying the first wave of marines and soldiers. Within minutes MacArthur was handed reports. His troops had landed and the Japanese had fallen back, their strategy soon to become clear: to retreat slowly toward the mountains of northern Luzon for a last-ditch stand, their backs to the sea.

At two that afternoon MacArthur climbed down a ladder onto a pitching launch that would carry him to the beach. He could have been put ashore on a dock. He firmly said no. He knew that the photos of him splashing ashore at Leyte had been spread across front pages and that American movie theaters had resounded with cheers as millions watched newsreels of him proclaiming, "I have returned!"

He ordered the launch to stop some distance from the shore. Then, as at Leyte, he waded ashore onto the Luzon he'd fled three years earlier.

"His Leyte wading scene was unintentional," wrote D. Clayton James, "but this one seems to have been a deliberate act of showmanship . . . . the Barrymore side of MacArthur's personality could not resist another big splash of publicity and surf."

He waded onto the beach as cameras clicked and whirred. Back home people thrilled as they read in their newspapers that "MacArthur is on his way back to Bataan." As he rode in a Jeep to a headquarters his staff had set up in the town of Dagupan, Filipinos lined the road and cheered. Some rushed up to him and kissed him. "It embarrassed me no end," he wrote later.

With General Krueger in command, the Americans and Australians pushed halfway to Manila within twelve days after the landing. MacArthur prodded Krueger to go faster. He wanted to seize Manila in order to cut off the Japanese before they could get to the mountains. And he wanted to free the thousands of American civilians and soldiers imprisoned in Manila before they were killed or crippled by captors MacArthur knew to be brutal.

The Japanese retreated slowly. Their rearguard occasionally threw fierce counterattacks. On the morning of January 28 one American unit, the 161st Infantry Regiment of the 25th Division, was caught offguard by a counterattack. The Americans turned and fled the fury of the Japanese assault.

MacArthur—who visited the front daily in his Jeep—drove by and saw the fleeing soldiers. He ordered his driver to stop. He and the regiment's commander, Colonel James Dalton II, stood shoulder to shoulder as they rallied the soldiers to stand and fight. Seeing Dalton and MacArthur, the American GIs did rally. The charging Japanese were met by a hail of fire, then by an attack that drove them back. A few weeks later, in another firefight, Dalton was killed.

The drive to Manila was still too slow for MacArthur. On January 30 he ordered two "flying columns" of First Cavalry Troops, one commanded by General Eichelberger, the Buna hero, to take off on a twenty-mile dash into the city.

"Go to Manila," MacArthur told one of his generals. "Go around the Nips, bounce off the Nips, but go to Manila. Free to internees. . . ."

One flying column, made up of tanks and armored cars, bolted into Manila. It clanked down streets as the astounded Japanese fled.

The tanks smashed through the front gate of Santo Tomas University and freed about four thousand American and Allied civilians who had been jailed there, sick and starving, for three years.

On February 7 MacArthur entered Manila and drove to the university. As his Jeep rolled by the smashed gates, the sunken-cheeked former prisoners surrounded him, cheering. They yelled "Thank you, thank you!" One woman, in ragged clothes, held her small child close enough to MacArthur to touch him. MacArthur was shocked to see the glazed look in the starved child's eyes.

MacArthur drove to Old Bilibid Prison, where eight hundred soldiers, some the men of Bataan who had lived through the Death March and three years of starvation on skimpy food "full of worms," had been freed. When MacArthur entered the prison, his eyes moistened. "The men who greeted me were scarcely more than skeletons," he later wrote.

He was told that some of his Bataan men waited to be inspected by their general. He walked into a steamy-hot, metal-roofed hut. His former soldiers stood as erect as they could; MacArthur stared solemnly at them—their faces bearded and wasted, their pants dirty and patched, toes sticking out of battered shoes.

He walked slowly down the line. As he passed one man, the soldier said, "You're back." Another said, "You made it." A third blurted, "God bless you."

Holding down his emotions, MacArthur could only reply, "I'm a little late, but we finally came."

Near the end of the line stood a man in dirty long underwear. He hobbled forward. He was a major who had fought on Bataan. "Awfully glad to see you, sir," he said, saluting. "Sorry I'm so unpresentable."

MacArthur shook his hand. "Major," he said with a taut smile, "you never looked so good to me."

The city of Manila had become a battleground. It was defended by twenty thousand Japanese marines and sailors, barricaded behind the stone walls of the Intramuros, the old walled city, who were determined to die rather than surrender. After a month of street-to-street fighting the Americans and Australians wiped out the last Japanese, only a handful surrendering. The artillery duels killed an estimated hundred thousand Filipinos trapped in their houses around the Intramuros.

While that battle raged, American paratroopers dropped onto the island fortress of Corregidor and some thousand marines swarmed ashore from landing craft. For ten days the Americans blasted five thousand defenders out of the labyrinth of caves and tunnels on the Rock with grenades, bazooka shells and flamethrowers.

Finally, on March 1, organized resistance was over on the Rock. The island had been captured at a cost of two hundred ten American dead. On the morning of March 2 MacArthur walked to a Manila dock. Striding with him were Generals Sutherland, Willoughby and all the others he could find who had fled with him from Corregidor that dark night in March, 1942. MacArthur and the other stepped into four PT boats, the same number that had carried them away from Corregidor three years earlier. In the bright sunlight the boats streaked across Manila Bay and tied up at a dock on Corregidor.

As MacArthur stepped onto the dock, a colonel saluted him and said, "Sir, I present to you Fortress Corregidor."

MacArthur returned the salute. It was a moment, he later wrote, "filled with drama and romance." He walked across the rocky Topside and looked downward toward Malinta Tunnel, where he and his family had lived during those months of continual bombardment. He saw where General Skinny Wainwright had come out of the tunnel with a white flag to surrender the men of Corregidor.

The marines and paratroopers were massed on the parade grounds. MacArthur, seeing the old flagpole still standing, turned to their commander and said, "Have your troops hoist the colors to its peak, and let no enemy ever haul them down."

144

During the next few months two armies, one commanded by Krueger and the other by Eichelberger, eradicated the remainder of the Japanese on Luzon, the other islands of the Philippines, and on additional major islands, including Borneo and Java. The Allied casualty lists would be long—eight thousand Americans and Aussies died to free Luzon alone. But the Japanese left more than two hundred fifty thousand dead in the Philippines. For every one of MacArthur's soldiers who died, thirty-two Japanese soldiers fell. MacArthur did not have a role in the bloody conquest of Okinawa, another of those "stepping-stones" on the way to the main Japanese islands.

In the spring of 1945 the war in Europe ended, Hitler's armies crushed between the armies of Russia and Eisenhower. In Washington and London Allied strategists began to plan for a mammoth invasion of Japan.

That invasion would take place—but without a shot being fired. A small band of Americans would land in Japan, followed—only two days later—by MacArthur. His plane would set down at Atsugi airport. Years later Churchill declared, "Of all the amazing deeds of bravery of the war, I regard MacArthur's personal landing at Atsugi as the greatest of the lot."

16

Surrender on the *Missouri*

"But you can't do that, General!"

General Eichelberger's words had a pleading tone while he glared at MacArthur. "At least," said Eichelberger, "give me two days to deploy my troops."

MacArthur only smiled. No, he said, he was going to Atsugi. His *Bataan* would set down on the runway shortly after Eichelberger had landed with his troops and completed taking over the airport.

But there were those suicide pilots, Eichelberger said. "At least," he pleaded, "give me two days" to guarantee MacArthur's safety.

"He gave me two hours," Eichelberger later said ruefully.

During the summer of 1945 the Air Force's new B-29s had bombed Japan's major cities and left many ablaze. Civilian deaths were enormous. Then came two final blasts—one that consumed Hiroshima on August 6, the other that obliterated much of Nagasaki on August 9. Uncalculated additional Japanese men, women and children died in these final great attacks, the world learning for the first time of the awesome power of the atomic bomb.

The official capitulation of the Japanese government had occurred on August 15—V-J Day. In Washington a new American President, the bespectacled Harry S. Truman—President Roosevelt had died in April—ordered two days of national celebrating. In Manila MacArthur—joined now by his wife and son—was swept up in a triumphal procession through the streets. They joined a worldwide party celebrating the end of World War II that had consumed many millions of lives. As Jean MacArthur rode in a car with her husband, she looked up and saw row after row of B-29s thunder over Manila. Remembering Corregidor, she said to her husband, "It's good to see our planes up there again."

On V-J Day MacArthur received an order from Truman appointing him the Supreme Commander for the Allied Powers (SCAP). As such he would command the forces which would occupy Japan. MacArthur's staff began to make plans to accept the Japanese surrender.

A Japanese delegation flew to Manila, where they conferred with Dick Sutherland. They were told to prepare Atsugi airport near Yokohama for the arrival of the first wave of American troops.

The Japanese begged Sutherland not to land at Atsugi. It had been a training base for the suicidal Kamikaze pilots. Outraged by the surrender, some diehards had killed their commanding officer and fired on the home of Japan's prime minister. When the Japanese were told that General MacArthur would land with almost the first American troops, they were horrified. They told Sutherland they could not guarantee that the Kamikaze pilots might not try to kill MacArthur.

Sutherland and Eichelberger suggested to MacArthur that he go to Japan aboard the battleship *Missouri*. "There are three hundred thousand Japanese troops around Yokohama," MacArthur was told. "You will be guarded by only a few hundred of Eichelberger's troops."

No, insisted MacArthur, he would land at Atsugi—and within hours after Eichelberger's advance troops. He knew the Japanese, he said, from his visit to that country with his father nearly a half century earlier. There was a national tradition, he said, that protected peaceful visitors against treachery. And he believed that his bold entry into Japan would impress the Japanese people. He could begin to change them from what their warlords had made them—a nation of warriors

On the cloudless morning of August 30, MacArthur kissed Jean and Arthur good-bye and boarded the *Bataan*. It flew north over the shimmering Pacific. During the five-hour trip to Japan, MacArthur paced the aisle and dictated a memo to his aide, General Whitney, outlining his plans for the defeated Japan. Some of them were based on what his father had told him of his experiences as military governor of the defeated Philippines.

"First destroy the military power," he dictated to the scribbling Whitney. "Then build the structure of representative government. . . . Enfranchise the women. . . . Free the political prisoners. . . . Liberate the farmers. . . . Establish a free labor movement. . . . Encourage a free economy. . . . Abolish police oppression. . . . Develop a free and responsible press. . . . Liberalize education. . . ."

At two o'clock, as the sun glared off the white runways at Atsugi, the *Bataan* curved down from the blue sky and rolled to a stop. In double rows facing the plane as its four engines coughed to a stop were Eichelberger's helmeted troops. Rifles and machine guns were clutched in their hands as they stood rigidly at attention.

Eichelberger stepped forward as MacArthur put foot on Japanese soil. MacArthur shook his hand and said, "Bob, from Melbourne to Tokyo is a long way, but this seems to be the end of the road. As they say in the movies, this is the big payoff."

General Whitney came off the plane and looked around nervously. He wondered if he would see a fanatical last charge by the suicide pilots. "I held my breath," he later said.

MacArthur climbed into a battered limousine which carried him the twenty miles toward Yokohama. The car bucked and backfired, the explosions causing the nervous Americans inside to reach for their pistols.

Then they saw the massed Japanese troops. Rifles gripped in their hands, they stretched in a long line on each side of the road. They stood with their backs to MacArthur's car.

They stood ready to protect him, MacArthur realized. And their turned backs were a sign of respect—the same token of respect that they showed for their Emperor. As MacArthur had guessed—and gambled on it with his life—the tradition of obedience had won out over the hatred of MacArthur instilled in the Japanese by the warlords.

All across Japan and China, meanwhile, American prisoners were being freed. Among those freed from a camp in China was General Jonathan Wainwright, who had surrendered on Corregidor. In Yokohama, MacArthur ordered that Wainwright, whom he called Jim, should be flown to Japan for the ceremony of surrender to take place in Tokyo Bay on the battleship *Missouri*.

MacArthur was seated at a dining-room table at his hotel in Yokohama when an officer told him that General Wainwright had just entered the lobby. MacArthur jumped up and strode to the lobby. There he saw an emaciated, pale, bent Wainwright, leaning on a cane. His new tan uniform flapped on his gaunt body, his eyes were lusterless after almost four years of near-starvation. MacArthur rushed forward and embraced him, saying over and over in a choked voice, "Jim . . . Jim. . . ."

He brought Wainwright with him to his table. There Wainwright told MacArthur that he feared he would be court-martialed for having surrendered.

MacArthur looked his old Bataan commander in the eyes and said firmly, "Jim, you can command any one of my corps that you want."

Only then did Skinny Wainwright realize that he had come home a hero. Soon he would be awarded the Congressional Medal of Honor for his leadership on Bataan and Corregidor.

A few days later, on the warm and cloudy Sunday morning of September 2, 1945, Wainwright and several hundred other gold-braided Allied generals and admirals stood at attention on the deck

149

of the *Missouri*. The gray battleship swung at anchor in the calm of Tokyo Bay. From its foretop fluttered the American flag that had floated over the U.S. Capitol in Washington on December 7, 1941, the "date which will live in infamy," as President Roosevelt had called it and that would now be avenged.

An eleven man Japanese delegation boarded the *Missouri*. Some were dressed in top hats and formal striped pants and looked like American undertakers. They walked to a table on the *Missouri's* deck and stood there silently under the gaze of thousands of sailors, photographers and war correspondents who were crammed onto the decks above.

Four minutes later the top commanders of the Pacific war— MacArthur, Nimitz and Halsey—strode out of a cabin and walked to the table. MacArthur spoke into a microphone to millions of Americans listening on their radios. One of the Japanese noticed that MacArthur's hands trembled with emotion as he said:

"We are gathered here, representatives of the major warring powers, to conclude a solemn agreement whereby peace may be restored. . . ."

He spoke for several minutes, then beckoned to the Japanese chief delegate to step forward and sign the instrument of surrender. With General Wainwright at attention behind him, MacArthur signed his name to the paper that formally ended World War II. The sun suddenly burst from behind clouds as Allied fighters and bombers swept overhead in a thunderous roar.

The Supreme Commander of Japan walked back to his cabin while the Japanese delegates filed off the deck, heads bowed. As General Willoughby wrote later: "The General had defeated the Japanese in battle. Now . . . he was to win them in peace."

But that peace would be splintered by the roaring of guns from a place only a few hundred miles from Tokyo Bay—Korea.

17

Caesar of Japan

The Emperor of Japan walked hesitantly into the room. He stood under the glittering chandeliers of the ornate, palacelike American Embassy in Tokyo. He faced Japan's Supreme Commander, General MacArthur, who was simply dressed in his open-necked tan shirt and pants, the five gold stars on the collar points. The Emperor was dressed in a diplomat's formal pants and coat with tails. He stepped forward and the two shook hands for the first time, MacArthur towering over the five-foot Emperor. He noticed that the Emperor's hands trembled with nervousness.

The first meeting was taking place a few weeks after the surrender on the *Missouri*. MacArthur thought that the forty-four-year-old Emperor had come to appeal for his life. In Washington, London and Moscow there had been demands that the Emperor be hanged for war crimes. But after interviewing a number of Japanese generals, MacArthur was convinced that the Emperor had not known of such brutal crimes as the Bataan Death March.

The Emperor and MacArthur sat down on a couch in front of a fireplace. Flames leaped and crackled around the logs as the two talked, their words translated by an interpreter who hovered above them. MacArthur offered the Emperor a cigarette, then lit it. The Emperor expressed his thanks in a shaky voice. Then he said:

"I come to you, General MacArthur, to offer myself to the judgment of the powers you represent as the one to bear sole responsibility for every political and military decision made and action taken by my people in the conduct of the war."

MacArthur stared, surprised, as the Emperor stopped and puffed nervously on the cigarette. The Emperor, MacArthur realized, had not come to beg for his life. Instead, he had offered his life to spare his people any punishment. "He was an Emperor by inherent birth," MacArthur later said, "but in that instant I knew I faced the First Gentleman of Japan in his own right."

A few minutes later, the Emperor left. As the visitor went through the door MacArthur felt even more certain that he should not be tried as a war criminal (and he never was). In a message to President Truman, MacArthur wrote: "For years the Japanese people have been led by warlords who instilled in them a fanaticism for war. Now we must count on the Emperor to lead them into the opposite channel—a fierce desire for peace."

Shortly after the Emperor left the American Embassy, where the MacArthurs now lived, the General told Jean about their conversation. "Oh, I saw him," Jean said, laughing. "Arthur and I were peeking behind the red curtains."

Each morning MacArthur awoke about 7:30 "in a house that was near bedlam," according to General Whitney, who had succeeded the retired Sutherland as MacArthur's chief aide. The General shaved with the three family dogs yapping at his heels. Then he chased the growing Arthur, a pale and fragile-looking boy, around the rooms in a wild-and-woolly free for all. He still doted on Arthur. Once, when the boy broke an arm while ice skating, MacArthur insisted that the Army doctors show him Arthur's X rays to be sure they had correctly treated the break.

During breakfast MacArthur read the newspapers. He read the

sports pages avidly, and each fall pored over news of Army's football team. He wrote to the Army coach, Red Blaik, to suggest plays for Army's quarterbacks. Each Sunday during the season he got a telephone call from an aide who flashed him the news whether the Army team had won or lost.

At exactly 10:30 each morning, seven days a week, MacArthur strode out of the embassy and stepped into a black limousine which sped him to an office building in downtown Tokyo as Japanese policemen bowed and switched traffic lights to green so the Supreme Commander would not have to stop. At the Dai Ichi office building, his headquarters, MacArthur strode up the steps while a huge crowd of Japanese watched silently. Any fanatic could have fired a shot at him—but no one ever did. Instead, men bowed and women sometimes prostrated themselves. MacArthur—by being the remote and mysterious Supreme Commander—had appealed to the Japanese reverence for authority. "The Japanese people themselves," he often said, "will protect me from assassination." They would never, he knew instinctively, slay a demigod. In their minds—and perhaps more and more in his own—he was half-god.

His top-floor office was austere (the windowless room had been used as a storage area). The only furniture was a desk, usually bare and without even a phone, a couch and a few chairs. On the walls hung portraits of Lincoln and Washington.

There during the next five years he ruled Japan's eighty million people. He passed on the judgments meted out to Japanese war criminals. Among those hanged was the warlord, General Tojo, and General Homma, whose troops had bayoneted Americans and Filipinos on the Bataan Death March. Some forty-two hundred Japanese were tried, with about seven hundred of them sentenced to death.

The bombardments had left millions of Japanese men, women and children wandering on streets and roads without homes or food. MacArthur ordered ships, filled with rice and other foodstuffs, to come to Japan from Australia and the United States. He oversaw the construction of new cities on scorched wastelands. And he made it easy and profitable for Japanese businessmen to open their factory doors to some seven million former soldiers who clamored for jobs.

He prodded Japan's Diet, the equivalent of the American Congress, until it passed a new constitution that set up a democracy. That constitution renounced war. For the first time Japanese women could vote. The Diet passed laws that gave land to farmers who had been virtual slaves of landowners. For the first time since the country had come under militaristic control Japanese workers could join unions.

MacArthur ordered the immunizing of all children against diseases that had once killed thousands of babies each year. Within a few years the life expectancy of Japanese men had been raised by eighteen years and by thirteen years for women. That was an achievement, an American doctor later said, "unequalled in any country in the world in medical history."

By the 1950s Japan's factories were cranking out cameras, cars, radios, phonographs, TV sets and other products to be shipped around the globe. "Made-in-Japan" products soon were famous for being both cheap and reliable. During the ensuing years Japan became one of the richest industrial nations of the world. Its workers were so busy that hardly anyone was ever jobless. Its currency, the yen, was soon among the strongest in world banking.

Over the years from 1945 to 1951 MacArthur changed the face of Japan. A ruffian dictatorship led by generals and admirals had become a busy and peaceful industrial democracy with the Emperor as its figurehead. And its people had changed from fierce warriors to contented workers.

"It is universally agreed,' one MacArthur biographer, Clay Blair, Jr., has written, "by journalists and scholars . . . that MacArthur and the officers and soldiers under his command did an excellent job of demilitarizing and democraticizing the nation. It was probably the most successful occupation of a major defeated power by its victors in the history of the world."

MacArthur's daily office routine was interrupted by lunch. At around two in the afternoon he sped back to the embassy. When he arrived, if there were luncheon guests, Jean would say, "Oh, here's the General." In public she always called him the General or, laughingly, "Sir Boss," never Douglas. "I guess you're hungry," MacArthur would usually say to the guests. "I know I am. Let's go and eat." And without any other fuss, everyone sat down.

But, eating only sparingly, MacArthur did most of the talking at those lunches. One guest, the writer John Gunther, later said: "What struck me most was his lightness, humor and give and take . . . one is apt to forget how human he is. I expected him to be oracular, volcanic and unceasing. He was all of that, but something else too: he laughed a good deal, enjoyed jokes, told some pretty good ones, permitted interruptions, and listened well."

But with closer friends and subordinates, MacArthur could take the stage and speak for hours without halt. He made biting comments on the European battles of Ike Eisenhower, who in 1946 had become the Army's Chief of Staff. MacArthur quoted British Field Marshal Viscount Alanbrooke, who had said after the war: "MacArthur was the greatest general and the best strategist that the war produced. He certainly outshone Marshall, Eisenhower and all the other American and British generals."

Some of his visitors suggested to MacArthur that he might be President of the United States. Republicans wanted him to run against Harry Truman in the 1948 elections. In private he put down Truman as "a hat salesman," which he once was, and called him Jewish, which he wasn't (there was a streak of anti-Semitism in MacArthur that also showed when he referred to Roosevelt as "Rosenfelt").

In public he claimed to have no interest in running for the Presidency. Yet he obviously wanted to be President. He seemed to say: "I want to be President, but I won't chase after it, you'll have to hand it to me."

In March, 1947, for example, he said: "While it seems unnecessary for me to repeat that I do not actively seek . . . any office, and have no plans for leaving my post in Japan, I can say . . . that I would [not] shrink . . . from accepting any public duty to which I might be called by the American people."

His ego had been stung—and he'd been embarrassed—in 1944 when he had seemed to lunge for the Presidency only to find there weren't enough voters who wanted him to be President. He had obviously decided not to look foolish a second time.

By early 1948 MacArthur for President clubs had sprung up across the United States. The owner of a chain of newspapers, William Randolph Hearst, printed huge headlines almost daily, AMERICANS CLAMOR FOR MACARTHUR! But that wasn't true. Many Americans seemed to think of MacArthur as so vain or pompous or simply so remote—he hadn't been in America now for almost a dozen years—that he wouldn't be "for the little man or the working guy in the factory." The feisty, tough-talking Truman was more the folksy kind of leader they wanted. Truman had once sold hats in his own Kansas City, Missouri, store (and gone bankrupt), but had risen to become an honest and hardworking judge, Senator, Vice President and President.

In the summer of 1948 MacArthur won only a few delegates to the Republican convention. The convention nominated Thomas E. Dewey to run against Truman. In that fall's election Truman gave fiery speeches around the nation as audiences shouted, "Give 'em hell, Harry!" Harry did—and beat Dewey.

MacArthur tried to disguise his disappointment at not being nominated by the Republicans. He had never had any desire to be President, he assured visitors. "I had not the slightest desire to become head of state," he later wrote, "having had enough of such an office in the administration of Japan."

That was a startling and revealing statement. MacArthur was saying that he was Japan's head of state. But he wasn't. As the Supreme Commander for the Allied Powers he was obeying the orders of Truman and other heads of state.

MacArthur obviously thought of himself as Japan's ruler. He lived in a castlelike home (it even had a moat in front of it). After five years of being fawned upon by aides like Courtney Whitney and being bowed to by the Japanese, MacArthur may have seen in his mirror what millions of Japanese saw: a demigod.

Also, more and more, he dwelt darkly on his "enemies in Washington." The man he considered his worst enemy, General Marshall, would soon become Truman's Secretary of Defense, the boss of the Army, Navy and Air Force. His former aide, Ike Eisenhower, was Chief of Staff and he was sure that Ike disliked him (they'd met only once in a dozen years, in 1946 in Tokyo, and talked icily to each other). And now he was sure that Truman held a grudge against him because some Republicans had wanted MacArthur for President. "From that moment on," he later wrote gloomily of the 1948 election, "it only became a question of time until retaliation would be visited on me."

While MacArthur remade Japan, he occasionally looked at what was happening across the Sea of Japan in the divided nation of Korea. A mountainous peninsula, it had been formally annexed to Japan in 1910. After the war Russian troops had occupied approximately its northern half, American troops the remainder. Its population of some thirty million had been divided into two countries—North Korea, where a Communist state was set up by Koreans loyal to Communist China and its then-ally, Russia; and South Korea, which was ruled by Dr. Syngman Rhee, a former professor. The boundary was the 38th parallel, originally established to separate the occupation zones. After 1945 the wartime friends, Russia and America, had drawn apart in what would be called the "Cold War." There was no hot shooting, but each side was suspicious that the other would attack. In 1949 Dr. Rhee pleaded with America to send arms to build up his Republic of Korea against an attack from "the North Korean Communist aggressors." Answering one of those appeals, MacArthur promised to send help to Rhee if he were attacked. Truman, however, never gave Rhee a firm yes or no answer.

In early 1950 MacArthur and his intelligence chief, General Willoughby, began to get reports from agents that the North Korean Army was massing along the 38th parallel. Willoughby predicted that North Korea would attack, but later changed his mind and said war was not imminent.

At dawn on June 25, 1950, North Korean shells rained into South Korean outposts. The North Koreans swept across the border into South Korea, scattering the poorly trained Republic of Korea (ROK) army. Low-flying Russian-built MIG-15 fighters strafed the fleeing ROKs.

At that moment MacArthur slept in his bedroom at the embassy in Tokyo, some five hundred miles away. As it had some nine years earlier, on December 7, 1941, the phone rang to awake him with the news that he was soon to command American troops in another war, for MacArthur his last.

18

The Guns of Wolmi-do

The phone rang for the third time in the dark bedroom. MacArthur, blinking, reached over and lifted the phone from its cradle. He heard the voice of a headquarters officer:

"General, we have just received a dispatch from Seoul advising that the North Koreans have struck in great strength south of the 38th parallel at four o'clock this morning."

MacArthur rose and was driven in the dark to his headquarters. there he learned that the hundred-twenty-thousand-man ROK army was being blown away by more than two hundred thousand crack North Korean troops. He also learned that fateful decisions were being made in New York and Washington.

In New York the United Nations Security Council met to discuss the invasion. The United Nations had been established shortly before the end of World War II as a place where nations could talk over their arguments. After a long debate, the Security Council called on all nations to "render every assistance" to South Korea.

In Washington President Truman toyed with his steel spectacles as he sat at his desk and grimly pondered what assistance he should render. He was sure the Russians had prodded the North Koreans into a grab of South Korea. The Russians, Truman believed, would see if the North Koreans could get away with this flagrant theft of a neighbor's land. If they did, the Russians would wind up another puppet and send it marching against yet another neighbor, Truman believed. He told his advisers that the Russians and North Koreans had to be stopped in South Korea to teach Communism the lesson that America and other peaceful countries wouldn't be pushed around.

In Tokyo, meanwhile, MacArthur decided to fly to South Korea to watch the battle. As he had said in France thirty-odd years earlier, "I can't fight the enemy if I don't see him."

On the morning of June 29, four days after the invasion, MacArthur walked toward the *Bataan* at the Tokyo airport through rain. His pilot, Major Tony Storey, stared upward at heavy clouds. "Sorry, General," he said. "The weather between here and Korea is too stormy for flying."

"We'll go," MacArthur said crisply.

Storey began to argue. MacArthur was insistent: they would take off. Finally Storey snapped: "I'll only risk your life, General, if you give me a direct order."

"This is a direct order. We'll take off."

Three hours later, after a storm-tossed flight, the *Bataan* circled a smoking Seoul, the capital of South Korea, then nosed down toward a shell-pocked airstrip. Minutes earlier a flock of North Korean bombers had ripped the field. As the *Bataan* jounced onto the runway, two North Korean fighters swept low over the other end of the field, strafing. They didn't spot the *Bataan* and flashed away.

Still nimble at the age of seventy, MacArthur hopped out of the *Bataan* and climbed into a Jeep. He was driven toward Seoul—right into the jaws of the advancing North Korean juggernaut. The Jeep stopped on the bank of the Han River. On the other side Seoul burned as enemy troops poured into the city. MacArthur lit his corncob pipe, took off his leather jacket in the humid heat and stuffed it under his arm as he walked to the top of a small hill.

There he stood for almost an hour to watch a scene of panic and flaming devastation, calmly puffing his pipe, his jacket still jammed under his arm. Around the hill below him swept frightened ROK troops and weeping civilians, clothing and possessions on their backs. MacArthur realized that the North Koreans could roll south from Seoul to the port of Pusan, on the tip of Korea only a hundred eighty miles away. Within a few days they would possess all of South Korea.

MacArthur drove back to the *Bataan* and took off as North Korean troops rolled to within a few miles of the airstrip. He cabled a report to President Truman, who read it carefully at his desk in the Oval Room of the White House.

Five years in the Oval Room had toughened "Give-'em-hell Harry." Truman had a favorite expression: "If you can't stand the heat, get out of the kitchen." He meant that if one couldn't bear up under the weight of making hard decisions, one should quit the job.

Truman made his hard decision. It was one that MacArthur applauded. Thus the President "accepted," as MacArthur later put it, "Communism's challenge to combat in Korea." Truman ordered MacArthur to send American troops to block the North Koreans.

This was the birth of the United Nations Army in Korea. Commanded by MacArthur, most of its troops were Americans or South Koreans, but there were sprinklings of soldiers from Great Britain, New Zealand, Australia and other nations. Truman called his sending of American troops a part of "a police action by the United Nations" to "render assistance" to South Korea. It was not the Korean War but "the Korean conflict," the U.S. itself never declaring war on North Korea.

In Japan MacArthur decided on a risky strategy as he assigned units to Korea. Most of his troops had been trained to occupy Japan and had no combat experience. But MacArthur decided to throw them in front of the advancing North Koreans in small units. He hoped that the North Korean commander, seeing American troops, would assume they were the spearhead of a much larger force. MacArthur wanted the North Koreans to stop and assemble their army for a massive punch at the Americans. And while the North Koreans halted, MacArthur could build up a line of defense around Pusan. That small ring, he hoped, could hold off the heavier force of North Koreans until fresh troops came from America.

The tactic worked—but at a terribly bloody price. Young American soldiers stood behind machine guns on Korean roads and were slaughtered by the North Koreans. Entire American companies of two hundred men vanished in a morning's fighting. The North Koreans could have swept by these tiny units and smashed into Pusan. But the North Koreans stopped, as MacArthur had hoped, and the Americans and ROKs had the time to form the defense ring.

But then the North Koreans slammed into the Pusan defenses. Slowly, step by step, they pushed the U.N. Army toward the sea. MacArthur begged Washington for reinforcements. He was quickly informed that there would be none.

Truman and his advisers did not want to fly American troops from Europe to Korea. They feared that the blow at Korea was only a feint by Russia. The real blow, they suspected, might fall on western Germany and France, garrisoned by more than a million Americans. If those troops were sent to Korea, western Europe's defenses would be wide open for a Russian onslaught.

In Tokyo MacArthur paced his office, furious that he again wasn't getting help. "Nothing has changed in Washington," he angrily told his staff. "To them Europe always comes first, Asia second." And Truman, he muttered, "has no definite policy in Asia."

MacArthur looked for help from the nearby island of Formosa. That onetime Japanese possession seized from China was now filled with a half million troops of Generalissimo Chiang Kai-shek. The generalissimo and his troops had been driven out of the Chinese mainland by the Chinese Communists. They hated the Communists, MacArthur pointed out, and would eagerly join the U.N. Army to fight the North Korean Communists. In America many people began to clamor for Truman to "unleash" Chiang's troops against the North Koreans.

Again Truman said no. He feared that if Chiang's troops stormed through the North Koreans and swept toward the Yalu River border with Communist China, the Chinese Communists would become alarmed. Millions of Red Chinese would pour across the Yalu, Truman said. And Russia—armed now with atomic bombs—might join its Chinese allies against the United Nations. That would begin World War III and destroy the world.

MacArthur argued—in cables to Secretary of Defense Marshall and in interviews with writers—that Truman and his advisers were overly worried. China and Russia, he claimed, would never start World War III to win a jagged piece of rock called Korea. And he began to tell his aides that some of the men around Truman, notably the highly patriotic Secretary of State Dean Acheson, were sympathetic to Communist China, Russia and Communism.

In the summer of 1950, as the Pusan ring shrank and Americans feared that nearly fifty thousand of its young men would be pushed into the sea to drown, MacArthur was asked to send a message to the annual meeting of the Veterans of Foreign Wars. His message was critical of those who, as he put it, "advocate appeasement and defeatism in the Pacific." Newspapers said that the message was a slap at Truman and his advisers.

Truman was enraged. MacArthur, he said, had become more than a general or Supreme Commander; he had become—or thought he had become—the equal of his commander in chief. "His lips white and compressed," according to one aide, Truman thought about firing MacArthur. "But after weighing it carefully," he later wrote, "I decided against it . . . I had no desire to hurt General MacArthur personally."

By the late summer of 1950 MacArthur's U.N. Army of almost a

163

hundred thousand Americans and ROKs had been pushed close to the Pusan beaches. In Tokyo MacArthur decided on a bold stroke. With a pointer he showed his staff how the North Koreans were feeding their two hundred thousand troops around Pusan. The line of supply ran several hundred miles from North Korea through Seoul to Pusan. Cut that line of supply, MacArthur said, and the North Koreans around Pusan—starved for food and ammunition— would have to pull back toward North Korea.

MacArthur jabbed the pointer at the port of Inchon, twenty miles west of Seoul. If we land here, he said, we could seize Seoul and cut the North Korean line of supply. And then——

His staff got the idea. If one U. N. Army stood in Seoul and another stood at Pusan, they would have the North Koreans trapped. Like giant hands, the two U.N. armies could come together with a clap that would smash the North Koreans between them.

MacArthur sent the idea to Washington. Quickly there came back reasons why the Inchon landing wouldn't work. Where would he get the troops to land at Inchon? asked the Joint Chiefs of Staff in Washington. MacArthur replied that he would train troops in Japan to land from the sea. And, in secret, he would pull some of his troops out of Pusan and have them take part in the landing also.

The Navy's admirals didn't like the idea at all. *Land at Inchon!* They sucked in their breaths in alarm. As one said, "If I had to pick one place in Korea that was the worst spot for a landing from the sea, it would be Inchon."

They had many reasons for opposing a landing at Inchon. There were the weird tides. High tide filled the Inchon harbor for as little as two hours. When the tide ran out to sea, the Inchon harbor became a big saucer of flat mud. Sure, said the Navy, we could sail into Inchon on the high tide. But we would have to capture Inchon within two hours. If we didn't, our ships and soldiers would be left mired in the mud to be annihilated by the guns of Wolmi-do.

Wolmi-do is a fortress island that stands over Inchon, to which it is connected by a causeway. It is ringed by fourteen-foot-high slippery

164

stone walls which the invaders would have to climb. Then the invaders would have to silence Wolmi-do's guns—all within two hours, before the tide ran out and mired the invasion fleet in the harbor's mud.

MacArthur still insisted that he could land at Inchon. The Joint Chiefs of Staff sent General Joseph Collins, the new Army Chief of Staff, and the Chief of Naval Operations, Admiral Forrest Sherman, to talk him out of the landing.

The three men, along with other high-ranking officers, sat at a long table at MacArthur's headquarters in Tokyo's Dai Ichi office building. The stubby Admiral Sherman spoke first. He ticked off all the reasons why a landing was impossible. He mentioned the tricky channels into Inchon and the treacherous tide. "If every possible geographical and naval handicap were listed," he concluded, "Inchon has 'em all."

Then the wiry Army general, Joe Collins, spoke. Why not attack the North Korean line of supply at an easier landing spot? he suggested. He named the port of Kunsan.

"I could feel the tension rising in the room," MacArthur later wrote. He lit his corncob pipe. As the smoke rose, he presented his case.

"Surprise is the most vital element for success in war," he said in his orator's ringing voice. Because Inchon appeared to be the worst possible place to land an army, he said, that would be where the North Koreans would least expect to be hit.

He stared at Admiral Sherman. He was sure that the Navy could land troops in Inchon. With light sarcasm in his voice he said, "I seem to have more confidence in the Navy than the Navy has in itself."

Then came a final argument. If the guns of Wolmi-do were not captured within two hours, he himself—aboard a ship with the invasion fleet—would call back the troops and landing craft before they were stuck in the mud.

He stared at the men around the table. "The only loss then," he said bitingly, "will be my professional reputation. But Inchon will not fail. Inchon will succeed. And it will save one hundred thousand lives"—the lives of the men with their backs to the sea at Pusan.

Sherman and Collins went back to Washington, and a week later the Joint Chiefs cabled their approval of the Inchon landing.

On the night of September 12, MacArthur walked up the gangway on the cruiser *Mount McKinley.* It sailed out of Japan into the buffeting winds of a typhoon that tossed the invasion fleet for two days. Worry creased the face of a seasick MacArthur. A few days before this invasion armada of forty thousand men had sailed toward Inchon, MacArthur had been given a message from the Joint Chiefs that "chilled me to the marrow of my bones." The message questioned the wisdom of withdrawing troops from the Pusan ring to sail to Inchon. But those troops, MacArthur knew, were needed at Inchon if the attack was to succeed.

"Had someone in Washington lost his nerve?" MacArthur wondered to himself. "Could it be the President? Or Marshall . . . ?"

But MacArthur was well aware that he had taken a terrible risk in pulling those troops out of the Pusan ring. On the night before the invasion, as the ships moved through the blackness toward Inchon with their lights out, MacArthur paced his cabin. With Courtney Whitney as his silent listener, he spelled out all the reasons why the Inchon landing might indeed become a nightmare.

Suppose the North Korean commander at Pusan discovered that MacArthur had weakened his ring by withdrawing troops? He could hit the ring like a hammer on an egg and slaughter the thinned-out Pusan army. Then where would MacArthur be? The North Koreans could turn and march north to blast his army of forty thousand that had landed at Inchon.

And suppose the North Koreans were waiting for him behind the guns of Wolmi-do? They would easily hold off his attacking marines for two hours. Like whipped dogs, MacArthur's army would have to run for their boats to get out of the harbor before they were stuck ingloriously in the mud. If either disaster happened—a blow at Pusan, a repulse at Inchon—the war would be over. The North Koreans would be the swaggering victors.

MacArthur talked on as the ship rolled through the black waters. Had he been wrong about Inchon? Had Collins and Sherman and the entire Joint Chiefs of Staff been right? Was he too old to be a commanding general?

It was too late to turn back. Inchon was now only hours away. At two-thirty in the morning MacArthur finally said good-bye to Whitney and the self-doubts that assailed him. "Thanks, Court," he said, "Thanks for listening to me. Now let's get some sleep."

He climbed into his bunk. Whitney left the cabin. "No, there was no doubt about the risk," Whitney said later. "It was a tremendous gamble."

19

Flight to the Yalu

The thunder of the *Mount McKinley*'s guns awoke MacArthur. He looked at his watch. It was almost an hour until seven in the morning, H-hour, when the first wave of U.S. marines would swarm ashore to attack Wolmi-do.

MacArthur quickly dressed and strode to the cruiser's bridge. With binoculars he watched Navy jet fighters swoop toward Wolmi-do. From the big ships that lined the shore streamed shells and rockets.

At seven MacArthur saw the first wave of black-hulled landing craft churn toward shore and vanish into the Flying Fish Channel that snaked into Inchon harbor. With each ticking minute the tide was emptying the harbor; in two hours his troops would have to flee or be slaughtered as they wallowed on Inchon's mud flats.

MacArthur paced the bridge. He saw hundreds of assault boats go into the Flying Fish Channel. Were they piling up behind a first wave of marines pinned down by sheets of fire?

Near eight o'clock a marine climbed the ladder to the cruiser's bridge. He saluted MacArthur, then handed him a slip of paper.

MacArthur scanned it. The message was from Inchon and it was simple: The marines had landed without losing a single man. The surprised North Koreans had fled. The marines had scaled the walls of Wolmi-do on special ladders. Its guns were silent.

MacArthur turned to the skipper of the *Mount McKinley*. "Please send this message to the fleet," he said with a smile. "The Navy and the marines have never shone more brightly than this morning." Then MacArthur walked off the bridge, saying to an aide, "Let's go down to breakfast." A night of anxiety had ended in a morning of triumph.

That afternoon MacArthur rode into Inchon and was driven some three miles inland. On the roads he saw Russian-made tanks and artillery abandoned by the fleeing North Koreans. By now more than forty thousand troops of his X Corps had landed at Inchon.

At the Pusan beachhead a hundred eighty miles to the south, the North Korean army began to retreat as it looked over its shoulder at X Corps rushing down atop them. MacArthur's Eighth Army swept out of their Pusan trenches to chase the fleeing North Koreans northward—right into the arms of the descending X Corps. On the morning of September 26, only eleven days after the Inchon landing, the soldiers of X Corps and Eighth Army shook hands. They had closed the trap on the North Koreans. More than a hundred thirty thousand were captured. Only a few remnants escaped across the 38th parallel into North Korea.

In one stroke MacArthur had destroyed an army that stood on the verge of triumph. Cabled President Truman: "Few operations in military history can match . . . the brilliant maneuver which has now resulted in the liberation of Seoul. . . . I salute you, and say from all of us at home, 'Well and nobly done.' " A few critics called MacArthur lucky at Inchon but most historians now agree that Inchon was MacArthur's greatest triumph.

In North Korea, however, stood another army. The head of the Joint Chiefs of Staff, General Omar Bradley, ordered MacArthur to cross into North Korea to "complete the destruction of the North Korean armed forces."

But at the United Nations there were demands by Great Britain and Russia that MacArthur stop at the 38th parallel. Many American and British diplomats worried that a thrust northward through North Korea toward Red China's border might bring millions of Red Chinese swarming into the battle.

MacArthur insisted on crossing the 38th parallel. "Unless and until the enemy capitulates," he told Secretary of Defense Marshall, "I regard all of Korea as open for our military operations." His two armies, the Eighth Army on the west coast and his X Corps on the east coast, thrust northward toward Pyongyang, the capital of North Korea, which was only about a hundred miles from the Red China border.

In Washington Truman worried about what would happen if the Chinese met American troops on the battlefield. Abruptly, he decided to have a face-to-face meeting with MacArthur. Up till then the two had never met.

Wake Island in the Pacific, about two thousand miles from Japan, was picked as the site for the conference. On the morning of October 15, 1950, the President's plane, the *Independence*, roared into Wake. MacArthur had arrived a few hours earlier on the *Bataan*. Dressed in his usual khaki pants, floppy hat and open-necked shirt, he stepped forward to greet the President. He shook the President's hand but did not salute. The Commander in Chief was annoyed. "I was sorry," Truman said later, "because I knew it meant I was going to have trouble with him."

MacArthur was relaxed, perhaps even contemptuous of this former Kansas City hat salesman. He had conferred with Hoover and Roosevelt when this slight man in the steel spectacles and Stetson hat was an unknown judge.

"I've been a long time meeting you, General," Truman said with a pleasant smile.

"I hope it won't be so long next time," MacArthur replied. But this meeting at Wake would be their last.

170

They climbed into a car. As it carried them to Truman's quarters, the President mentioned the coming election in 1952. MacArthur, Truman later wrote, said he was not interested in politics. Politicians had made "a chump" out of him in 1948, Truman recalled him saying, but that would not happen a second time.

An hour later the two men conferred in a cigar-shaped tin-roofed hut. Truman had brought with him almost a dozen military, diplomatic and political advisers. With MacArthur was only General Courtney Whitney.

MacArthur pulled out his corncob pipe. "Do you mind if I smoke, Mr. President?"

"No," said the grizzled politician. "I suppose I've had more smoke blown in my face than any other man alive." MacArthur and the other men laughed.

For most of the next hour and a half the men at the table discussed what would happen in Korea and Japan after the end of the war. MacArthur predicted that the war could be over by Thanksgiving or Christmas, only a month or two away. Near the end of the conference Truman leaned forward on the table and asked MacArthur what the chances were that the Chinese would plunge across the Yalu River into North Korea.

"Very little," MacArthur replied. He explained why: The Chinese troops would be cut down by American bombers and fighters as they crossed the jagged mountains of North Korea.

The meeting over, MacArthur and Truman drove to the airport. On the way MacArthur asked Truman if he intended to run for reelection in 1952. Truman smiled. He had dodged that question from reporters for months. He ducked it again by asking MacArthur: What were the general's political ambitions?

MacArthur smiled. "None whatsoever. If you have any general running against you, his name will be Eisenhower, not MacArthur."

Truman chuckled. As events unfolded, MacArthur turned out to be right. In 1952 Ike Eisenhower did run for the Presidency on the

171

Republican ticket—not against Truman but against Adlai Stevenson—and won.

Back in Tokyo, MacArthur directed the drive of his two armies, X Corps commanded by General Edward Almond, Eighth Army by General Walton Walker. MacArthur dropped paratroopers behind the North Koreans, hoping to trap them. That drop helped to capture Pyongyang on October 22 and MacArthur landed there in the *Bataan* next morning. But he learned that the North Koreans had slipped through the nets of his trap.

Their escape infuriated MacArthur. Washington had ordered him not to send American troops into the northern reaches of Korea, where they would skirt the Red China border along the Yalu. He was only supposed to send ROK troops. But he ordered Walker and Almond to push north. He explained glibly to Washington that this was "a matter of military necessity."

Truman and his military and diplomatic advisers were aghast as they began to realize they had lost control of MacArthur. At Inchon he had been right and they had been wrong. And Inchon had made MacArthur a miracle man to millions of Americans. Truman and his advisers sat back and hoped the Chinese would not intervene.

But Chinese armies had massed along the Yalu. Their leaders issued a warning that the approach of the U.N. army was "a serious menace to China." And in Tokyo MacArthur's intelligence officers read reports that Chinese troops had already entered North Korea and clashed with ROK units.

At first MacArthur seemed too intent on destroying the North Korean army to see the storm warnings. Early in November Washington cabled him: Were the Chinese about to attack? His answer was: He doubted it.

On November 6 he shocked Washington with a "special communiqué" to the world that announced the entry of Chinese troops into North Korea. MacArthur denounced the intervention as "international lawlessness." He ordered his bombers to smash every "factory, city, village" to blast the Chinese out of North Korea.

172

As part of that massive assault by air, MacArthur told his bomber pilots to knock out the bridges over the Yalu River. Then, he figured, no more troops or supplies could flow from China into North Korea.

Truman and Marshall, back in Washington, were alarmed into action. They feared that bombs might fall on Red China, killing civilians, an act of war. MacArthur was told not to bomb any target within five miles of China. MacArthur angrily retorted that he had to bomb the bridges to cut off the Chinese troops flowing into Korea. "Your instructions," he almost insolently told his commander in chief, "may well result in a calamity of major proportions."

MacArthur—inflated by his successes as a general and his stature as a godlike ruler to the Japanese—had forgotten the most basic of all rules for a soldier: to obey orders.

After much debate in Washington, MacArthur was told he could bomb "the Korean end" of the bridges. But his B-29s, as they neared the Yalu, were swooped on by Chinese fighters, which peppered them with shells, then fled back across the Yalu. The Chinese knew that American jet fighters were not allowed to chase them into Chinese territory.

MacArthur demanded the right of "hot pursuit" into China. This time Truman and his advisers were adamant: No. MacArthur and his pilots were understandably outraged. MacArthur later wrote, perhaps more emotionally than accurately, that a dying bomber pilot, his arm blown off, had gasped to him, "General, which side are Washington and the United Nations on?"

"For the first time," MacArthur told his staff, "a commander has been denied the use of his military power to safeguard the lives of his soldiers." But he watched with growing satisfaction as his fleets of B-29s darkened the skies over North Korea to pour down thousands of tons of bombs. After two weeks he was sure he had obliterated the Chinese armies in North Korea.

He ordered his two armies to leap toward the Yalu, the offensive to begin on November 24, the day after Thanksgiving. Once more

Truman, Marshall and Acheson nervously wondered: What would the Chinese do as the U.N. Army drove toward their doorstep? They told themselves that MacArthur might end the war by Christmas—and without the Chinese coming in.

But MacArthur himself was worried about the Chinese. On Thanksgiving Day, a few hours before the offensive, he visited his front-line troops in North Korea and told the marines and soldiers that they might be home by Christmas. Then he climbed into the *Bataan* and told Major Storey to head north toward the Yalu.

General Whitney stared, unbelieving. The *Bataan* was unarmed. It could easily be picked off by the Chinese MIGs that swarmed around the Yalu. But MacArthur insisted: He had to see the enemy.

The plane droned over the barren, jagged landscape and came to the winding Yalu. From his seat MacArthur stared down intently. From horizon to horizon he saw only a stillness frozen by howling wintry winds from Manchuria. Nothing moved.

No, MacArthur reassured himself, the Chinese no longer flooded into North Korea. And his bombers had erased the Red China army that had been there.

He was wrong. Almost two hundred thousand Chinese had hidden in deep mountain passes while bombs rained around them. Now they crouched in those mountains, poised to ambush the onrushing X Corps and Eighth Army.

20

"Going Home at Last"

The two generals strode down the long hallway. Their black combat boots clacked loudly on the white marble. They were dressed in battlefield uniforms—helmets, baggy green jackets and pants. Only hours before they had flown from the roar and smoke of the battlefield in North Korea as their armies reeled backward.

A servant swung a door open. The generals—they were the tall Ned Almond and the stubby Walton Walker—entered a large room. In front of a fireplace, hands jammed deep into his back pockets, strode MacArthur. He looked dejected.

Some twenty hours earlier more than two hundred thousand Chinese, their bugles blaring, had swept out of North Korea's mountain passes to overwhelm Almond's X Corps and Walker's Eighth Army. At this moment the Americans and ROKs carried their dead and wounded on stretchers as they retreated southward into biting near-Arctic cold and whipping blizzards.

From North Korea war correspondents cabled their newspapers that this defeat at the Yalu was "America's worst defeat ever." On their still-new black-and-white TV sets, Americans saw glazed-eyed and bandaged American soldiers stumble down North Korean hills, faces wrapped to protect themselves against the fierce cold.

In the ornate, chandelered room at the American embassy MacArthur conferred with Almond and Walker through the night. They agreed to try to pull back X Corps and Eighth Army to ports where they could be evacuated to South Korea.

MacArthur tried to put the best face on the retreat. He called war correspondents into his Tokyo office and told them he had not lost at the Yalu—he had won. Cunningly, he explained that he had "sprung the Chinese trap and escaped it." Had he not sprung the trap, he said, "we would have been a sitting duck" doomed to eventual annihilation.

Why, asked the correspondents, hadn't he known about the Chinese ambush? He had a quick explanation: He blamed Washington. Their global intelligence should have warned him that the Chinese would attack. And he hinted to reporters that "Communist sympathizers" in the State Department had tipped off the Chinese to his every move.

He brushed aside the heavy losses at the Yalu—almost thirteen thousand South Koreans and Americans killed, wounded or missing. That was "half the losses at Iwo Jima," a Navy operation, he noted. And with a swipe at an old rival, he added that those thirteen thousand casualties were "even less in comparison to the Battle of the Bulge," Eisenhower's defeat in World War II.

He seemed almost desperate to restore the image of the victorious Inchon general. He blamed Truman for the ambush. Truman had forbidden him to bomb Chinese bases across the Yalu, he said, "an enormous handicap without precedent in military history."

Reading what MacArthur had said, Truman fumed. "I should have relieved General MacArthur then and there," he later wrote. "The reason I did not was that I did not wish to have it appear as if he were being relieved because the offensive had failed. I have never believed in going back on people when luck was going against them. . . ."

X Corps and Eighth Army were evacuated to South Korea and set

176

up a defensive line across the waist of South Korea. In setting up that line, General Walker was killed. He was replaced by Lieutenant General Matthew B. Ridgway, a front-line general like the now-retired Bob Eichelberger. Matt Ridgway stalked the front lines with hand grenades strapped to his chest and a pistol on his hip.

Ridgway conferred with MacArthur in Tokyo. He felt MacArthur looked discouraged by the war he had thought he had won at Inchon and now seemingly had lost at the Yalu. Ridgway asked MacArthur: "Do you have any objection to an attack?"

"The Eighth Army is yours, Matt," MacArthur said almost listlessly. "Do what you think best."

At first Ridgway's Eighth Army was pushed backward toward Pusan. But by early March, 1951, it had counterattacked, recaptured Seoul, and stood at the 38th parallel where the war had begun some nine months earlier.

"Perfect," said Truman's staff. "The North Koreans are back in North Korea and the South Koreans have their country." Why not, they suggested to Truman, ask the Chinese to withdraw and end the bloodshed?

In Tokyo MacArthur heard that kind of talk and said he was appalled. "We had lost our will to win," he later wrote. The attitude of President Truman, Acheson and Marshall, he said, had "deteriorated into defeatism. This is something new for our nation. In war there can be no substitute for victory."

Truman wanted peace without victory. MacArthur wanted peace only with victory. That head-knocking debate began to split the nation—just as it would during another undeclared war, in Vietnam, some two decades later.

On March 20, 1951, the Joint Chiefs cabled MacArthur to inform him that Truman would soon invite the Chinese to a peace conference. Four days later MacArthur defied an order from the Joint Chiefs of Staffs to issue no communiqués without their approval. He did issue one, and it was like a bucket of cold water

177

thrown into the faces of the Chinese whom Truman was trying to lure to the peace table. The MacArthur communiqué taunted the Chinese for "their exaggerated . . . military power." It promised a new offensive that "would doom China." But MacArthur offered to confer with the Chinese generals to end the war.

That statement was all Truman could take. MacArthur had taken on the role of commander in chief by dictating to the enemy the terms of war and peace. "By this act," Truman later said, "MacArthur left me no other choice—I could no longer tolerate his insubordination."

On the morning of April 6 Truman sat down behind his desk in the Oval Room with Secretary of Defense Marshall. The silvery-haired Marshall could remember how arrogantly MacArthur talked to superiors from Marshall's days on Black Jack Pershing's staff in France. He told Truman that MacArthur should have been dismissed two years before.

Truman asked Marshall to see what the Joints Chiefs—the Army, Navy, Marine and Air Force commanders—thought he should do. Their answer was unanimous: Relieve MacArthur of his command. Truman nodded when Marshall told him. But he had already made up his mind to fire MacArthur no matter what the Joint Chiefs would say.

To make the firing as gentle as possible, Truman instructed Marshall to contact an Army official who was at the front in Korea. The official was to fly to Tokyo to give MacArthur a message from the President that he was dismissed.

But a Chicago newspaper, the *Tribune,* heard of the firing. The *Tribune* was about to publish the story. So that the news would come first from the White House, Truman's press aide hastily called reporters to his office at one o'clock in the morning on April 11. A few hours later Americans read this statement from Truman on the front pages of their morning newspapers:

"With deep regret I have concluded that General of the Army

Douglas MacArthur is unable to give his whole-hearted support to the policies of the United States Government and of the United Nations. . . . I have, therefore, relieved General MacArthur of his commands and have designated Lieutenant General Matthew B. Ridgway as his successor."

In Tokyo—the time there around two in the afternoon—Colonel Sid Huff had been listening to a radio news broadcast when the announcer broke in with the flash from Washington. At that moment Jean MacArthur happened to phone Huff. Huff told Jean what he had just heard.

"Is it true?" she asked.

Yes, said Huff, he was sure it was true.

Jean MacArthur walked to the dining room, where MacArthur was having lunch with guests. She walked behind him and tapped him on the shoulder. She bent down and whispered to him the news of his dismissal.

"MacArthur's face froze," one witness later wrote. "Not a flicker of emotion crossed it. For a moment, while his luncheon guests puzzled on what was happening, he was stonily silent. Then he looked up at his wife, who stood with her hand on his shoulder."

"Jeannie," MacArthur said in a firm voice, "we're going home at last."

21

"Old Soldiers Never Die"

The *Bataan* droned across the night sky over San Francisco Bay. MacArthur had wanted to arrive in America—for the first time in fourteen years—late at night. "That way," he told Courtney Whitney, "we will be able to slip into a hotel without being noticed."

Some twelve hours earlier his plane had lifted off from Tokyo and he had looked down on Japan for the last time in his life. As he rode to the airport an estimated one million Japanese had packed the streets to wave good-bye with tiny American and Japanese flags. Later the Emperor would award MacArthur the Grand Cordon of the Order of the Rising Sun with Paulownja Flowers, the highest Japan can give to a foreign head of state.

With MacArthur on the *Bataan* were Jean and Arthur, who was now thirteen. As the plane swung down toward the lights of San Francisco, MacArthur put a hand on Arthur's shoulder and said, "Well, Arthur, my boy, here we are at home at last."

The plane rolled down the runway and stopped. MacArthur stepped out of the door and saw several thousand people massed behind police lines. Among them was California Governor Earl Warren. They roared out a welcome. On the highway, as the

MacArthurs drove into San Francisco, more thousands packed the curbs to cheer and wave. They were the first of millions of Americans who were about to give MacArthur a salute that was perhaps the most emotional in this nation's long history of welcoming home its heroes.

In almost every home, office, shop and factory Americans argued with each other. Some loudly said Truman was wrong in firing MacArthur; others said just as loudly that he had been right. On the floors of the houses of Congress Senators and Representatives demanded that Truman be impeached. Others called him courageous. That debate still goes on among some who remember the shock felt by Americans at news of the firing of MacArthur.

To MacArthur the firing was proof of his long-held belief that he had "powerful enemies behind me in Washington and elsewhere." He claimed that bells pealed in Moscow and Peking at the news of his dismissal. And he said that his old enemy from the Chaumont crowd, George C. Marshall, had finally finished him. "The President let George do it," MacArthur told intimates. "Whoever was on the firing squad, it was George who pulled the trigger."

From San Francisco the *Bataan* flew the MacArthurs to Washington. MacArthur had been invited to address a joint session of Congress, an honor usually given only to Presidents and visiting heads of state. (Some Washington jokesters said this made sense: Wasn't MacArthur a visiting head of state?)

At a little after noon on April 19, 1951, he stood high on a rostrum to address the Congress and a packed gallery that included his proud wife and son. He wore his creased suntan pants and shirt, his only decoration the five stars on each side of his collar. Across the nation some twenty million Americans watched him on their television sets—one of the largest TV audiences up to that time. They saw the approximately six hundred Senators and Congressmen rise and applaud him for some five minutes. When the tumult finally faded, he calmly sipped from a glass of water and then began a speech that, even decades later, is still recalled with choked throats by many who heard it.

He began by describing how Communism was threatening Europe and Asia. He said he was no lover of war. "I know war as few other men now living know it," he said, his voice resonant in the hushed chamber, "and nothing to me is more revolting." There must be an end to war, he said, or mankind would perish.

But, on the other hand, he said, ". . . once war is forced upon us, there is no other alternative than to apply every available means to bring it to a swift end. War's very object is victory. . . . In war, indeed, there can be no substitute for victory."

And he added that Red China had to be stopped in Korea. "For history teaches us with unmistakable emphasis," he said as Congressman stood to cheer, "that appeasement but begets new and bloodier war."

Then, as the seventy-one-year-old voice vibrated with emotion, he came to the end of his speech: "I am closing my fifty-two years of military service. When I joined the Army even before the turn of the century, it was the fulfillment of all my boyish hopes and dreams. The world has turned over many times since I took the oath on the Plain at West Point, and the hopes and dreams have long since vanished. But I still remember the refrain of one of the most popular barrack ballads of that day which proclaimed most proudly that 'Old soldiers never die, they just fade away.' "

The hall was still, every eye fixed on the old soldier. He smiled down at the rows of Senators and Congressmen and said slowly:

"And like the old soldier of that ballad, I now close my military career and just fade away—an old soldier who tried to do his duty as God gave him the light to see that duty. Good-bye."

He turned and stepped down. Congressmen rose to applaud. Across the nation people wept.

But this old soldier did not fade away for a long while. During the next few weeks he was hailed in cities across the country in one tumultuous parade after another. Millions in New York City roared to the trench-coated MacArthur as he waved from an open car and ticker tape swirled around him—a welcome that many still think was the most fervent in that city's many welcomes to heroes. "America," he later wrote, "took me to its heart with a roar that will never leave my ears."

A few Republicans asked him to run for President in 1952. This time he firmly refused. "I do not intend to run for political office," he said, "and I hope that my name will never be used in a political way. The only politics I have is contained in a single phrase well known to all of you—God Bless America!"

The Republicans nominated Eisenhower. In his campaign Eisenhower vowed to go to Korea to find a way to end a war that had become an artillery duel along the 38th parallel. He was elected and went to Korea in the late fall of 1952. Shortly after his return he and MacArthur met in the New York apartment of John Foster Dulles, soon to be Eisenhower's Secretary of State. It was only the second meeting between the two since then-Colonel Eisenhower had left MacArthur's staff in Manila in 1938.

The two talked briefly but with obvious coolness. Eisenhower knew that MacArthur had been envious and resentful of his rise to fame and power. And MacArthur disliked Ike as "one of Marshall's boys." But Eisenhower had been told that MacArthur had a plan to end the Korean war and he had asked to see it.

The plan was typically MacArthurian in its boldness. It suggested that the new President confer with Russia's leader, Josef Stalin, to agree to end war forever. If that agreement were not reached, then MacArthur proposed that the United States drop atom bombs on North Korea and China so that China could never war again.

Eisenhower thanked MacArthur. But as President he ignored the idea. He began negotiations with the North Koreans that finally resulted in a cease-fire and a peace. North and South Korea were again divided by the 38th parallel.

Many of MacArthur's admirers later argued that if China had been crippled as MacArthur proposed, the Red Chinese could not have planted Communist governments in North Vietnam and elsewhere. And then, they said, there would have been no bloody Vietnam war with its killing of more than fifty thousand young Americans. But others have said: If we had bombed China, Russia would have bombed us, consuming America and perhaps the world in an atomic holocaust.

MacArthur and his wife lived in a large and sumptuous apartment high in the towers of the Waldorf-Astoria Hotel in midtown Manhattan. MacArthur took a well-paying job as chairman of the board of the Sperry Rand Corporation, one of whose principal executives had been a long-time friend and admirer.

During the rest of the 1950s and on into the early 1960s he often addressed conventions of businessmen and veterans. He warned constantly against "Big Brother" government in Washington that was getting fatter on taxes taken from Americans as it told those Americans how to live their lives. Expressing the view of many American conservatives that the federal government had become dangerously powerful, he said: "The fundamental and ultimate issue at stake is liberty itself."

Several times during the 1950s he took teenaged Arthur with him to that place he loved—West Point. He smiled with obvious pride in his eyes as Arthur was photographed wearing a cadet's cap. But Arthur chose not to go to West Point and become the general his father and grandfather had been. He attended a civilian college and almost a hundred years of military service by the MacArthurs came to an end.

MacArthur had rarely been ill for more than a few days. But in 1960, just before his eightieth birthday, he was stricken by a glandular illness that almost killed him. When he came out of the hospital several months later looking pale and gaunt, an old Rainbow Division comrade asked him, "How does it seem to be so old?"

MacArthur smiled up from his wheelchair and said, "With my date of birth, if I were not old, I would be dead."

A few days later a man stopped him on a New York street as MacArthur strolled with a cane. The man told him he looked better than he had in recent newspaper photos. "Yes, sir," said the man, "your pictures do you a great injustice, Mr. Truman."

"I didn't know," MacArthur later said, "whether to laugh or cry."

His strength ebbing, he still was able, with the aid of Courtney Whitney, to write his memoirs, *Reminiscences*. In March, 1964, he entered the Army's Walter Reed Hospital in Washington. Reporters saw an ashen-faced shadow of a man slumped in a wheelchair that was pushed by his wife. A few days later he was wheeled into an operating room. After several operations on a diseased gallbladder, he died at 2:30 p.m. on the afternoon of April 5, 1964. He was eighty-four.

President Lyndon B. Johnson declared a state of national mourning. The body was first taken to New York for a funeral with full military honors. Then, on a rainy morning, the flag-covered coffin was placed on an artillery caisson and pulled by four horses through Manhattan's streets to the Pennsylvania Railroad Station. Behind the caisson trotted a white horse, riderless. In the softly falling rain the entire West Point Corps of Cadets—the long gray line in which he'd marched at the turn of the century—stood erect at attention. Sabers dipped in salute to the dead First Captain of the Corps.

The coffin rode by train to Washington. There it was placed in the Capitol rotunda, where the body of the slain President, John F. Kennedy, had been honored only a few months earlier. From the rotunda it was rolled by caisson to Arlington Cemetery, where Douglas MacArthur was buried next to his father.

MacArthur. How does one assess the man and the general? As a general he can be faulted for mistakes on Luzon and at the Yalu. But there was also Champagne-Marne, and the Ourcq, and Los Negros and the other Pacific landings of World War II, and then Inchon. Those are a litany of victories attained by no other American general over so long a period of time.

As a general and as a human being he was loved and admired by the people closest to him, from sergeants like DaTorre to generals like Kenney and admirals like Halsey. A few on his staff, like Eichelberger, saw the man's flaws but all had respect and awe that endured.

Historians and biographers, not awed by the closeness of his dominant presence, have painted portraits of a man who strove to be the giant he thought his father was. In straining to be that giant, MacArthur became obsessed with the need to be always right. Around him he gathered fawning men, like Courtney Whitney, who assured him he was always right. When he was wrong, "he had a desperate need to save face," to make himself look good, "even if it involved lying," D. Clayton James, has written. In the book he wrote on his life, *Reminiscences,* MacArthur barely ever—in over four hundred pages—admits to having made a mistake.

What was he really like? What, deep down, did he think of himself? Those are difficult questions to answer of any person, especially difficult to answer of a man hailed by adoring millions as a miracle worker, chieftain and near divinity.

But men don't usually lie about themselves when they know they are close to death and believe they will be judged by Almighty God. In May 1962, toward his end, MacArthur made a final visit to that place where he had left so much of himself—West Point (now a statue of him faces the Plain). His face was gray, his voice quavery, but he delivered to the assembled Long Gray Line probably his most beautiful of speeches. He told them—as Elihu Root had told him and his fellow cadets some sixty years earlier—that one day they

186

would be locked in war's savagery. "Only the dead," he told them somberly, "have seen the end of war." Like Root he was prophetic: within a few years some of those cadets would die in the rice paddies of Vietnam.

Then, in his closing words, MacArthur summed up in three words—"Duty, Honor, Country"—what were probably his firmest beliefs and the words he had lived by:

"The shadows are lengthening for me," the old man's voice quavered in the hushed hall of cadets. "The twilight is here. My days of old have vanished tone and tint; they have gone glimmering through the dreams of things that were. Their memory is one of wondrous beauty, watered by tears, and coaxed and caressed by the smiles of yesterday. I listen vainly, but with thirsty ear, for the witching melody of faint bugles blowing reveille, of far drums beating the long roll. In my dreams I hear again the crash of guns, the rattle of musketry, the strange mournful mutter of the battlefield. But in the evening of my memory, always I come back to West Point. Always there echoes and reechoes in my ears—Duty–Honor–Country."

The voice faded for a moment as the old general prepared his last salute to this place—and all it embodied for him.

"Today," the hollow voice said, "marks my final roll call with you. But I want you to know that when I cross the river my last conscious thoughts will be of the Corps—and the Corps—and the Corps.

"I bid you farewell."

Index

189